Arthur Crockett & Timothy Green Beckley

ANGELS of the LORD
Calling Upon Your Guardian Angel
for Guidance and Protection

Special Thanks to William Alexander Oribello

Expanded Edition Introduction By Sean Casteel

LET THERE BE LIGHT

INNER LIGHT PUBLICATIONS

ANGELS OF THE LORD

EDITORIAL DIRECTION
& LAYOUT
TIMOTHY GREEN BECKLEY

ANGELS OF THE LORD

Manufactured in the United States of America.

For information:

Inner Light Publications
Box 753
New Brunswick, NJ 08903

Mrufo8@hotmail.com

www.conspiracyjournal.com

<u>Prayer to Your Guardian Angel</u>

A prayer to say to Your Guardian Angel.

Protecting spirit who watches over me always, you who have this mission, now for the joy of doing good and for progress and purification of your spirit, save me; during the night my spirit goes to meet the unknown, take me to where my loved ones and my friends are, those who want to help me, help me with all the problems of my life. Oh, that the revelations I should put into practice would be held fast in my imagination.

Give me strength in my contemplation of nature and raise my spirit above the new struggles that have made my hopes vanish. Amen.

ANGELS OF THE LORD

Metaphysical artist Carol Ann Rodriguez renders visionary likeness of her Guardian Angel.

Contents

ANGELS OF THE LORD

Do They Have Wings?

Introduction To The Expanded Edition Of
"Angels Of The Lord"

By Sean Casteel

Most people are willing to pay lip service to the idea of angels, but few are ready to make that leap of faith and say they experience angels in real-world terms. Read stories of people whose very lives were saved by these normally unseen agents of God.

Ever wonder why angels are said to have wings? The late scholar Zechariah Sitchin, whose in-depth research into ancient religious myth knows few equals, explains how the iconic image of winged angels came to be.

If angels had not intervened, publisher, editor and writer Timothy Green Beckley would have gone "over the edge," so to speak, and this book would not be possible!

Did an angel appear from nowhere and spare rock guitar virtuoso Jimi Hendrix from a snowy, freezing death on the outskirts of Woodstock, New York, in 1965? Where would rock music be today without that apparent helping hand that allowed Hendrix to live on?

Abductees Raymond Fowler and Betty Andreasson Luca both hold firm to the belief that their contact experiences with "extraterrestrials" have been of an angelic nature. Why do they see the love of God manifested in what happened to them?

Much has been written about the dark side of the flying saucer phenomenon. Are you ready to read a more pleasant although an equally more challenging view of the moral character and abiding love of some of the UFO occupants?

Some of those reading our earlier collection "Round Trip To Hell In A Flying Saucer - UFO Parasites, Alien 'Soul Suckers' And Invaders From Demonic Realms," expressed concern over our postulation that "aliens" represented demonic armed forces sent by Satan acting as his advance troops to subject humanity to the darkest mental and physical anguish imaginable. We quoted such experts as Jacques Vallee as saying, "UFOs are real but they are not physical. They are messengers of deception," and that, "The UFO beings of today belong to the same class of manifestations as the (occult) entities that were described in centuries past."

We also noted a rather sensational statement in a Library of Congress publication about UFOs that, "A large part of the available UFO literature is closely linked with mysticism and the metaphysical. It deals with subjects like mental telepathy, automatic writing and invisible entities as well as phenomena like poltergeist manifestations and possession. Many of the UFO reports now being published in the popular press recount alleged incidents that are strikingly similar to demonic possession and psychic phenomena that have long been known to theologians and parapsychologists." The late Lord Hill Norton, former U.K. Defence Chief and head of the British Fleet, expressed the opinion that UFOs represented more of a religious phenomenon than a military problem.

But there is another side of the cosmic coin to consider. To simplify things, for those who accept a literal interpretation of Biblical text, God and his forces are not about ready to turn over and play dead. In the struggle for humanity, God has created his own legion of soldiers, some of whom may have craft they travel in which we call UFOs.

The internet site BibleUFO.Com/angel, which offers a "traditional Christian outlet on the web," lets even the most faithless amongst us gain a bit more knowledge of

the stature of angels and their connection with unexplained aerial and mysterious ground level phenomenon:

"Angels are the messengers and most physically present of the spiritual beings in the eternal world of the Elohim. The word used in the Old Testament is Malak, pronounced mal-awk' and means to dispatch as a deputy; a messenger; specifically, of God. They serve the Elohim, though obviously not in absolute perfection, as conveyors of thought and action. They are not gods. They are protectors of the Elohim and mankind. They are not described as having wings, halos, harps, or having the appearance of the orthodox portrayal as commonly seen in paintings and other representations. Angels can appear in flying vehicles or on terra firma and are often in some form of brilliant uniform. There are at least 2 ranks of angels with the archangels being superior in rank. Satan was, of course, an angel, apparently of very high rank though in earlier times he attempted to take over the throne of the Elohim.

ANGELS OF THE LORD

Angels appear almost 200 times in the Bible so the entries in this section deal with those references that relate to appearances in the sky, vehicles, and close encounters."

Our old friend and accredited journalist/investigator Brad Steiger takes perhaps a bit more secular view of what angels mean to us in the overall scheme of things to do with UFOs. He phrases it most excellently in his recently published "***Real Aliens, Space Beings, And Creatures From Other Worlds***": "There seems little question that for many people the space beings function as angels. They are concerned about Earth. They seem to be actively trying to protect it and the people in it. They are powerful. They avoid, or have control over, the physical limitations of time and space, yet they are benevolent and kindly disposed toward fumbling, bumbling, ineffectual humankind. It seems that space beings have placed themselves in the role of messengers of God, or that we, in our desperation for cosmic messiahs who can remove us from the real situation we have made on this planet, hope that there are such messengers who can extricate us from the plight we are in."

Though this is NOT a UFO book, it is a work in which we hope to prove that there are inter-dimensional beings coming here to assist not only the planet in its spiritual growth, but also to guide each one of us in our search for the meaning of existence and allow us to lead a beneficial life. Apparently, there is a struggle going on for the soul of humankind and a battle for the minds of man.

THE BATTLE FOR THE MINDS OF MEN

Born on the 17th of February, 1910, in the province of Alberta, Canada, Wilbert Smith joined the Department of Transport of Canada as its chief engineer at the age of 25. He worked mainly in the broadcasting field and deserved credit for advancing the technical aspects of broadcasting in his native country. During World War II he was responsible for the establishment of a network of ionosphere measurement stations and later set up several broadcasting agreements between Canada and the United States.

In December 1950 Smith successfully persuaded the Canadian government to set up a laboratory and field facilities to study UFOs, which were being seen in increasing numbers. For nearly four years he ran the semi-official Project Magnet in an attempt to understand and study the physical principles behind the unknown phenomenon. Because of the nature of his position, it is believed that Smith was called upon to examine the Roswell UFO retrieval wreckage. Later, once again in private life, he organized the Ottawa New Sciences Club, which became embroiled in a controversial study by those who maintained they had established communications with the beings responsible for the UFO phenomenon.

Smith engaged in an evaluation study comparing notes gathered from numerous UFO contactees whose sincerity he had complete faith in. He found similarities in their experiences about what the benevolent "space beings" had revealed to them in the way of universal wisdom and knowledge. Every single one of these contactees told of a cosmic battle between Good and Evil being played out both in the invisible realms and the physical world, pretty much the same - but in more "Space Age" terminology - as the Scriptures describe the war between Satan's demons and God's angels.

Wilbur explained this battle in the following manner: "I propose to (offer) a grave danger which we are all, consciously or unconsciously, facing in a world in which two great forces are striving to gain control of man's mind. This struggle has been going on from time immemorial, but never in the world's history has the conflict been more intense than it is in this present era of confusion and unrest. In the old days, mankind was often made to suffer physically, unspeakable things in the name of power, but today, with man's mind more developed and better educated, he is now facing the prospect of a refinement of even greater mental and spiritual cruelty - unless he is prepared to protect himself with right thinking.

"The two great forces," Smith continues, "involved in trying to influence man's thinking may be described as positive, i.e., thought in harmony with the concept of a love of Good and the brotherhood of man, and negative, those encompassing anti-Christ motives designed to gain control over man for the purpose of power. The battle of man's mind is being waged on two fronts, the physical and the metaphysical and the object of the fight is to bring about either the spiritual salvation or destruction of homo sapiens."

To add weight to the evidence of Smith's claim that there is a battle going on "upstairs" we refer readers to material presented in the aforementioned "Round Trip To Hell In A Flying Saucer" provided by Joshua Warren in the form of photos showing an aerial clash between UFOs and triangular-shaped craft in the darkness of space beyond our atmosphere which can be seen quite clearly through night vision goggles and which have even been filmed by our astronauts and are available on YouTube.

CALLING UPON YOUR PERSONAL GUARDIAN ANGELS

Will Smith is not alone when he contends that the "good guys" (the angels in Biblical fashion, or Space Brothers in UFOlogical terms) are beaming down positive energy to negate the negativity of our environment, and suggests we can join in the battle. "If there was a great outpouring of prayer and positive thought issuing from the inhabitants of our world, thus raising the spiritual vibrations of our planet, this would enable them to assist us further. . . The explanation given is that a large number of our Space Brothers (angels), whose special mission it is to safeguard the spiritual welfare and evolutional progress of Earthlings, had banded themselves together to form what might be described in Earth terms as a 'cosmic police force.'" This group - which many identify as the Watchers - maintains a steady effort to "keep at bay negative forces who attempt to inflict their stronger evil influence on negative and borderline-negative earthlings," and keep away any "dangerous forces" who are arriving in an attempt to drag us down into the cosmic sewer.

So as this book will demonstrate, we should extend good will and have compassion so as to radiate our light into the universe and help our angel friends keep at bay the forces of Lucifer, the fallen one, and his minions. This book is a clarion call for those who wish to attract positive benefits into their lives. Offered are several helpful ways to contact your own personal Guardian Angel. We will also relate various episodes of those whose lives have been saved or completely turned around by these benevolent beings who we can, say such experts as William Oribello, actually communicate with and ask to do our bidding.

According to author Malcolm Godwin, in his book "*Angels: An Endangered Species*" (Simon and Schuster, 1990), "The Angel is one of those Articles of Faith as unshakable as our belief in the existence of God, an atom, or the ill luck of the number 13. One in every ten popular songs invokes angels in some form. They appear on Christmas cards and wedding invitations, they abound as souvenirs, jewelry and religious or semi-religious bric-a-brac. Every museum is packed full of paintings and sculptures of these winged beings and artists and writers depict them to this very day.

"But ask anyone if they really believe in the existence of the angel," Godwin continues, "and suddenly a profound conflict arises between the unthinking certitude of a faith and the sophisticated realism of the current century."

With this book, we hope to add a little reinforcement to the belief that angels are an eternal and everyday reality for the people who need them and who are open to bringing the helpful love and support of the divine beings into their lives.

Defining exactly what an angel is is not a simple task. The word "angel" itself comes from a Greek translation of the original Hebrew word "mal'akh," meaning "the shadow side of God," which later came to mean "messenger" or "herald."

While simply tracing the origin of the word "angel" may leave us with only a vague understanding of the subject, the author of "Angels, True Stories Of How They Touch Our Lives," Hope Price, says that the Bible teaches us certain definite truths.

"Angels, according to the Scriptures, are unique spiritual beings who act as messengers and comforters to mankind. In Biblical times they were frequently reported to have been sent by God to give direction or help in time of difficulty to a wide variety of human individuals. They appeared mysteriously, either alone or in groups. They were seen, they spoke and sometimes they sang. Their appearance was awesome, and initially often frightening. After their missions had been fulfilled, equally mysteriously they disappeared.

"According to the Bible," Price goes on, "angels are an entirely different species from humans. It emphatically tells us not to worship them. No matter how thrilling an angelic visit may be, our praise should be only for God. Among the nearly 300 Biblical references to angels, some stand out, either because they were more dramatic or because they affect people's lives. For example, God sent an angel to shut the mouths of the hungry lions when Daniel was thrown into their den (Daniel 6:22). Elijah and Jesus were both fed by angels in the wilderness, when there was no food around (1 Kings 19:5-8; Mark 1:13). St. Paul, before he was shipwrecked, was sent an angel to convince him that he would survive (Acts 27: 21-26)."

But Price is also led to the same bump in the road as Godwin. While no one would likely question the existence of angels in the context of the Bible, making that leap of faith today is a little more difficult.

"In our modern era," she writes, "an aura of myth and make-believe surrounds the subject of angels. What seems normal and perfectly acceptable in Biblical terms seems irrational and impossible in our everyday lives. In effect, according to popular belief, all possibility of Divine intervention in our worldly affairs, through angels, is rejected."

ON THE WINGS OF ANGELS

The late researcher and author Zechariah Sitchin, whose groundbreaking series of books called "The Earth Chronicles" are considered definitive classics of ancient astronauts-type research, also grappled with our traditional concepts of what angels are and how they appear. Writing in a companion book to the series, "Divine Encounters, A Guide to Visions, Angels and Other Emissaries" (Avon, 1995), Sitchin tells us, "The popular notion of angels, an image sustained and bolstered by centuries of religious art, is that of fully anthropomorphic, humanlike beings who, unlike people, are equipped with wings. Indeed, were they to be stripped of their wings, they would be indistinguishable from humans.

"Brought over to Western iconography by early Christianity," Sitchin continues, "the undoubted origin of such a representation of angels was the ancient Near East. We found them in Sumerian art - the winged emissary who led Enkidu [an ancient Sumerian deity] away, the guardians with the deadly beams. We find them in the religious art of Assyria and Egypt, Canaan and Phoenicia. Similar Hittite representations were duplicated in South America, on the Gate of the Sun in Tiahuanacu - evidence of Hittite contacts with that distant place."

And again, Sitchin reminds us that the modern world continues to reject the notion of angels when discussing the ancient evidence. In contemporary scholarship, there seems to be a tendency to eliminate the word "angel" entirely and call the various religious icons by another name.

ANGELS OF THE LORD

"Though modern scholars," Sitchin explains, "perhaps wishing to avoid religious connotations, refer to the depicted beings as 'protective geniuses,' the ancient peoples considered them to be a class of lesser gods, a kind of rank-and-file divine being that only carries out the orders of the 'Great Lords' who were 'Gods of Heaven and Earth.' Their representation as winged beings was clearly intended to indicate their ability to fly in Earth's skies, and in that they emulated the gods themselves. In this regard, the Lord's statement (Exodus 19:4) that he would carry the Children of Israel 'on the wings of eagles' might have been more than allegorical."

KEEPING BABY SAFE

Editor, writer and publisher Tim Beckley has a made a life's work out of studying the paranormal and has encountered supernatural beings both positive and negative. From his childhood on, he says it is possible, though he has no way of proving it, that "something" - some energy - some being(s) - have been watching over him and guiding his life in the general direction of the strange. Beckley even has his own angel story to tell.

"As a child of three or four," Beckley began, "I had an experience with what I believe may have been a guardian angel or some other corporeal being. My father was raised in Kentucky, in the small town of Shelbyville, located about 30 or 35 miles from Louisville. It's the home of the king of fried chicken, Colonel Sanders. He was born and started his first restaurant in Shelbyville, and it is now one of the biggest franchises in the U.S."

Beckley's parents met and married in Kentucky, but soon relocated back to his mother's home state of New Jersey. His mother had asthma and other allergies, which were relieved by a yearly trip to Kentucky in the family Oldsmobile.

"In those days," Beckley said, "Kentucky was a place where you would go if you had problems breathing. No pollen and short grass. That's why they call it the Bluegrass State, the home of the Kentucky Derby."

Beckley's parents loaded up the car with supplies and made a makeshift little "hideaway" bed in the back seat for young Beckley. The trip was a long one, lasting three or four days. His father did most of the driving while his mother sat up front overseeing the situation, as mothers do. As the family neared its destination, they found themselves in the mountains with the hour growing late and a thick fog rolling in.

"My father insisted that they continue to drive," Beckley said, "because he was bushed and just wanted to get to where we were going. He didn't want to pull over and spend the night in the middle of nowhere. But my mother insisted to my father, 'You have to stop right now. Do not go another inch farther.' So by that time it was very foggy and they couldn't see ahead of them on the roadway at all. So they parked.

"The next morning," Beckley continued, "when the sun came up and cut through the fog, it turns out the vehicle we were in was on the cusp of going over the side of a mountain cliff. If they had driven another two feet, I would not be here today to tell you this story or to be the publisher of so many works on spiritual and paranormal subjects."

Beckley does not question the notion that something divine intervened for his family and himself that night.

"Of course, I can't prove it," he acknowledges, "but with all the other things that have happened in my life, there is a good possibility that angels and UFOs are related. I do believe that they are inter-dimensional beings and come from another realm. So it's quite possible that my life was actually saved by an 'angelic being' of some type so that I could carry out my life's work, which might in turn benefit their overall mission. I guess it wasn't my turn to go.

"Someone is sort of sitting 'up there,' to see that we don't end up dying before our allotted time. To do so might throw off the entire space/time continuum," he said in a tongue-and-cheek tone, no doubt having watched a fair share of "Twilight Zones" and science fiction movies where this time travel theme has frequently been played out and is often referred to as the "grandfather effect."

Beckley says he has no actual memory of the events himself. It was a story handed down to him and retold through the years within his family.

FOR THE LOVE OF ROCK AND ROLL

ANGELS OF THE LORD

But Beckley also says his favorite "angels saved me" story comes from Curtis Knight, a former member of the band The Squires, fronted by the late guitar virtuoso Jimi Hendrix. As recorded in one of Beckley's books, *UFOs Among The Stars*," Knight tells about a cold winter's night near Woodstock, New York, in 1965, years before the fabled music festival that would bear the town's name.

"It was four o'clock in the morning," Knight recalled, "and we were trying to make it back to Manhattan - a drive of more than a hundred miles - through the worst blizzard I can remember. The wind was whipping the snow around our van so fiercely that we missed the turnoff leading to the state highway that would put us in the direction of home. The next thing I remember is getting stuck in a drift that reached the hood of our vehicle. Soon it got so cold. The windows were rolled up tight and we had the heater on full blast to protect us from the rawness of the elements. I had my doubts about seeing the light of day. We could have turned to human icicles very easily. That's how bitter it was!"

The road in front of the imperiled musicians suddenly lit up, Knight said, and a bright, phosphorescent object, cone-shaped like a space capsule, landed in the snow about a hundred feet up ahead. It stood on tripod landing gear and looked like something right out of a science fiction film.

"At first, we thought it was an apparition," Knight said, "caused by the cold and our confused state of mind. I mean, we just couldn't believe our eyes."

Knight prodded Hendrix with his elbow and asked if the future superstar was seeing the object as well. Hendrix only smiled and seemed at that point to be staring out into the night. Three other members of the band were wrapped up in blankets and sleeping in the back of the truck. When Knight was unable to rouse them, he feared they might be suffocating from carbon monoxide fumes caused by the closed windows. Knight began to feel overcome with fear.

At that precise moment, a door opened on the side of the spacecraft and an entity came forth.

"He stood eight feet tall," Knight said, "and his skin was yellowish. Instead of eyes, the creature had slits. His forehead came to a point and his head ran straight into his chest, leaving the impression that he had no neck."

The being proceeded to float to the ground and glided toward the van. Then Knight noticed that the snow was melting in the entity's wake.

"His body generated tremendous heat," Knight recounted, "so much so that, as it came across a small rise, the snow disappeared in all directions. In a matter of what seemed like seconds, the being came over to the right hand side of the van where Jimi was seated and looked right through the window. Jimi seemed to be communicating telepathically with it."

The temperature in the van grew extremely hot very quickly, going from bitter cold one moment to a heat that made Knight feel like he was roasting. The entity from the UFO caused the snow around the vehicle to evaporate enough to free their trapped vehicle. Knight gunned the motor and drove away quickly. The road behind them began to fill in with snow again as the strange craft lifted off like a rocket from   a launching pad and disappeared.

Knight has since passed away, but he never stopped believing that a miracle had transpired that snowy evening and that he and Hendrix and the others were saved by a UFO. Hendrix apparently felt it wasn't "hip" to talk about what had happened, and the other musicians did not recall the incident at all. They remained asleep until the van reached the main road they had been seeking, prompting Knight to conjecture that they had been "hypnotized" or "under a spell" for the duration of the incident.

THE ANGELIC UFO "INVASION" OF EARTH-WILL THEY INTERVENE ON OUR BEHALF?

UFO and alien abduction researcher Raymond Fowler has pursued the truth of the flying saucer phenomenon since the 1950s, serving as chairman of the National Investigations Committee on Aerial Phenomena (NICAP) and authoring several books on the subject, including a series of books on the abduction experiences of devoutly Christian housewife Betty Andreasson Luca. Sometime in the 1980s, Fowler began to be aware that he was himself an abductee, with the same foggy memories of having been taken from his bed and brought onboard a ship as is commonly reported by thousands of other "experiencers." At one point during a dramatic regressive hypnosis session, Fowler began to cry.

In an interview I conducted with him for a 1991 issue of *"UFO Magazine,"* Fowler told me, "I rarely cry, and in the few instances that I have cried, it has been in private. I am known for my unemotional, logical approach to things. What made me cry under hypnosis was the overwhelming feeling of love that emanated from a shining being. It was so overpowering that I had to literally gasp out my words to the hypnotist and investigator. I was told that something wonderful was going to happen in the future and that I would in some way help it to happen. I can remember waking up that morning and still feeling the remnants of that wonderful feeling and trying to retain it."

Fowler said he had previously felt that same overwhelming sensation of love on several other occasions. It had happened once when he was lying in bed as a teenager and experiencing an emotional inner conversion to Christianity.

"It occurred again as a teenager," he said, "when I was about to do something which I knew was morally wrong. At this time, someone took over my mental facilities and spoke very kindly to me and the young lady who was with me. I had no control over what was coming out of my mouth. Basically, we were told why what we were planning was wrong. This incident terrified the young lady and made me feel very ashamed. The next time, it occurred when my wife and I were praying together shortly after our marriage."

It seems apparent that something angelic was guarding over Fowler, determined to see that he remained pure for his future wife, and making sure that he did not give into the standard temptations of adolescence. While the experiences may not involve a dramatic, lifesaving intervention, they are nevertheless moments of rescue and salvation that display a kindly guiding hand that reinforces its presence with an overpowering feeling of love and affection.

ANOTHER ABDUCTEE'S CONTACT WITH ANGELS

Betty Andreasson Luca was Raymond Fowler's primary research subject. She is a housewife who has been abducted by aliens throughout her life and has been a Pentecostal Christian from her childhood on. While it is often the case that conservative Christians view the UFO occupants as something demonic, Luca unflinchingly sticks to her guns that her alien contacts have been of an angelic nature.

In an interview for one of my previous books, "*UFOs, Prophecy and the End of Time*," Luca told me that she based this belief on her own encounters.

"Regardless of whether it is God's angels or lost, fallen angels," she said, "we humans are the battleground or territory either side wishes to gain. My encounters with benevolent beings have strengthened my faith in the reality of the seldom-seen world of the government of God. His messengers have been sent to do his will, and although I have seen and heard yet not always understood, I can rest in His promises and faith."

When I spoke to Luca again a few years later, her faith remained much the same.

"My UFO encounters with extraterrestrials," she said, "which I believe to be Angels or Messengers, have helped me to mature as a child of God. My Christian faith is of the utmost importance to me, and I believe it has occasionally given me access to a realm rarely seen by physical eyes. And yet this God-given rite of passage can exist for everyone, for the Creator is not a respecter of persons. His love for everyone is unconditional and encompasses all."

Luca says that affirming her faith was what led to her extraterrestrial encounters as an adult and added that, "While immersed in a benign celestial world filled with mystery, the angelic host began to reveal themselves little by little."

While contact with angelic extraterrestrials is something that could happen to anyone, it is important to be grounded in faith when exposed to their strange spiritual world.

"For once there," she cautioned, "you will experience what eyes have not seen and ears have not heard. For the unprepared, it can be a world of sheer terror. For when man neglects to know himself and his Maker, it leaves him open to fear."

The well-known abductee and author of "Communion" and its many sequels, Whitley Strieber, once commented on Luca to me.

"The number of us who are so spiritually superb as Betty," he said, "who can really make this encounter fly, is tiny. Most of us are down in the muck struggling with it. That's why Betty is such an inspiration to me. When I was at the depths of my depression, one of the things I did was read Betty's interviews and listen to her tapes, just to hear the sound of her voice. I would also look at drawings she sent me and it helped a lot. Betty's experiences are the thing you grab onto while you're sinking."

ANGELS OF THE LORD

Encounters With Human-Looking Angels
In Both Modern And Ancient Times

By Sean Casteel

- Does everyone have a guardian angel? You may be surprised to learn the answer is yes! Their presence is hard to quantify, but we'd be lost without them, according to former journalist Phil Krapf.
- Read how Biblical scholar Gary Stearman believes the angels of the Bible traveled in UFOs that crossed between dimensions and were the vehicle of Christ's ascension.
- A housewife and her two children are saved from certain death by an angel who looked like a young man but had the strength of a hundred men - a classic angel rescue story.
- The ancient Biblical story of Sodom and Gomorrah involves the appearance of two angels who looked indistinguishable from mortal men yet unleashed a deadly vengeance on the evil cities from the skies above. Perhaps such angels walk among us today?

AN ATHEIST FINDS A GUARDIAN ANGEL

Phil Krapf's story contains elements of both the standard contactee and abductee scenarios that have been widely reported for more than fifty years. He is a former journalist with the Los Angeles "Times" and even shared in a group Pulitzer Prize awarded to him and his coworkers for their coverage of the 1992 Los Angeles riots. His encounter experiences began after his retirement, and he had had no interest in the subject while at the newspaper.

Krapf awoke in the early morning hours of June 11, 1997, to find his bedroom bathed in an eerie kind of light. A beam of light focused on him and in the next split second he found himself standing in front of a group of strange-looking creatures. He described them as a cross between the typical gray aliens and something more human-appearing. Krapf states that his mind continued to function normally and rationally in spite of what was happening to him, and the aliens explained that the light had a calming influence on people.

21

The aliens explained that they were on the verge of establishing diplomatic relations with the governments of the Earth and were recruiting humans to serve as ambassadors to make the transition easier. As a former journalist, Krapf was being sought out to help them write a reference guide to create a bridge of understanding between the two races.

After Krapf had written a pair of books on his alien abductors and their plans to be recognized on Earth ("*The Contact Has Begun*" and "*The Challenge of Contact*"), a human-looking entity named Paul that Krapf had met onboard an alien ship came to him saying that Krapf needed "counseling."

"He was worried about my health," Krapf said. "I think that he quite frankly thought I was suicidal. I assured him that I was fine. I was depressed because of 9/11, as all Americans were. Sleeping pills and alcohol and tranquilizers and the sale of everything else like that went up. Americans were traumatized, and I was traumatized too."

Krapf and Paul met with one another for about 18 months, a time that included an out-of-body experience in which Krapf was taken to an alien cocktail party but was never quite sure if he was physically there.

"We're aboard a spaceship," Krapf said, "and we're with these strange creatures, and it's a social setting, a social situation. I was going back and forth between whether or not I was really there or whether my body was still stuck back on the patio, but I was there. My consciousness was there. That was one of the adventures we had."

Although Krapf was an atheist in the time he knew Paul, and continues to be one to this day, he has a possible explanation for Paul's spiritual benevolence.

"I wanted to know," Krapf said, "whether everybody has a guardian angel, and Paul said, yes, they do. It is easy to imagine that of all the billions of galaxies out there, some of them may contain star systems with planets like ours. And of those, maybe a thousand might have civilizations on them. And of those civilizations, there might be one in which the inhabitants have a full, long, rich life. But perhaps there is something missing. Perhaps they're unfulfilled.

"There are missionaries on Earth," he continued, "who go out to less fortunate people and minister to them. I was thinking that they would not necessarily minister to us, but let's say they are these very altruistic people who take it upon themselves to guide other creatures through their lives, to look after them, to guard them in some way. To me, that's not beyond the realm of possibility."

Krapf posed still another question to Paul: How much influence does a guardian angel really have on people's everyday lives?

Paul replied, "It's hard to quantify, but we're there. Sometimes we're there in periods of crisis, and other times we can not be available for months on end."

Paul suggested a method for demonstrating how necessary his help was: He would stay out of Krapf's life for a little while. The two agreed on a three month testing period. Krapf was immediately burdened by a series of obstacles that included being falsely accused in a hit-and-run driving accident and his bank somehow losing track of thousands of dollars from an account he maintained. Krapf said he was so stressed out from all the bad luck that he became emotionally debilitated. He finally had had enough and asked for Paul to return.

Paul also encouraged Krapf to try to develop his telepathic abilities, but Krapf came to feel he had no talent for it. Ever since Krapf submitted his manuscript on his contact with the guardian angel, which became the book "Meetings With Paul," Paul has not appeared to him in visible form.

THE RIGHTEOUS UFOs OF THE BIBLE

Gary Stearman has been a part of the Oklahoma City-based television ministry "Prophecy In The News" for well over twenty years. He has devoted himself to studying the scriptures, especially Biblical prophecy, as it relates to current events around the world. Stearman has definite views on angels and UFOs and the way the two phenomena are interrelated. I interviewed Stearman for a book I wrote called *"Signs and Symbols of the Second Coming"* and got his opinions on the righteous UFOs of the Bible.

"People who read the Bible," Stearman said, "believe in the literal existence of angels, that angels come and go, day by day, in our world, but they are not seen in general. They have some sort of an ability to be present without revealing themselves to human eyes.

"And in Second Kings, Chapter Six," he continued, "there's a wonderful example of that in which the prophet Elisha went out with his servant and they were camped out. It was a time when the Syrian army was coming against Israel. They woke up the next morning and Elisha and his servant discovered themselves to be surrounded by the Syrian army. And the servant said, 'What in the world are we going to do?' Then Elisha prayed and said, 'Lord, I pray thee, open his eyes that he may see.' The Lord opened the eyes of the young man and he saw, and behold, the mountain was full of horses and chariots of fire round about Elisha. In other words, these chariots of fire are the way the Bible describes what I regard as UFOs.

"If a chariot of fire," Stearman went on, "makes itself visible, such as the time when the prophet Elijah was taken to heaven in a chariot of fire, or in the first chapter of Ezekiel, when a chariot of fire came across the plain and landed right in front of Ezekiel, when these chariots of fire become manifest, they resemble nothing quite so much as what we call UFOs in the modern era. The servant of Elisha was simply allowed to see these fiery chariots, which means they're not far distant from us. There is perhaps a dimensional shift that allows them to conceal themselves."

Stearman also believes that when Jesus ascended into heaven in front of his disciples after his resurrection, the mode of transportation for Jesus was also a UFO.

"Here we see a couple of angels," Stearman explained, "describing to the apostles that Jesus would come in the same way that he left. The way he left is that a cloud received him up, and that cloud departed. I take it that this cloud was some form of celestial transportation vehicle. So to me, that explains much of what modern man sees when he's looking at UFOs. He's really seeing a glimpse of the spirit world when he sees the UFO."

A CLASSIC EXAMPLE OF RESCUE

In a book called "*Where Angels Walk*" (Ballantine Books, 1992), author Joan Wester Anderson presents a wonderful collection of real life angelic encounters. One is called "Rescue on the Tracks," and tells the story of housewife and mother Carol Toussaint.

Carol was driving her large station wagon across Arlington Heights, Illinois, about five P.M. on a hot summer weekday. She was going to pick up one son from his guitar lesson and her two other children were in the backseat. She was running late starting dinner and her mind was fixated on getting home as quickly as possible. She turned off the busy highway and onto a set of railroad tracks that intersect the downtown area. But before she could travel through the railroad crossing, her engine suddenly died. She was stuck, blocking several lanes, with her front wheels resting in the track grooves.

She tried several times to restart the car, but the ignition wouldn't catch. Cars began to honk behind her and brakes screeched as rush hour travelers attempted to go around her. Her children began to complain of the heat and confinement.

"It was a driver's worst nightmare," Anderson writes. "Suddenly a young man wearing a white shirt and tie loped casually over to Carol's open window."

The young man asked if she was aware that she was in danger. She answered that yes, her husband would kill her for being too late to make dinner on time.

"No, I didn't mean that," the young man said. "There's a train due through here in about half a minute. I'm going to have to move the car for you."

Carol then recalled that at that time of day, several commuter trains sped through the crossing at frequent intervals. Even if the next train was due to stop at the station a block or two away, it would still be moving too fast to avoid hitting her and the children. Carol can't recall what she did next because the panic she was feeling clouded her memory.

"But she'll never forget the reaction of the serene young man," Anderson continued. "Nonchalantly he walked to the front of her car and gave it a little one-handed push. The huge station wagon dislodged easily from the track grooves, and as the crossing gates came down and warning bells began to clang, it rolled back across the tracks and safely over a little incline, where it again came to a stop. Almost immediately, the train roared past. Stunned, Carol realized that, without the young man's help, her family would have been hit and killed. But where was he? The train had blocked her view for only a moment. How could he have disappeared in this open area without her seeing him?"

Later, mechanics and others arrived to push Carol's car down the rest of the incline to a nearby gas station. Although the man in the white shirt had dislodged the large vehicle with one hand, it took eight people to move it all the way across the highway.

"Carol's husband didn't get his dinner on time that night," Anderson concludes. "He received a far greater gift."

SEEING ANGELS IN HUMAN FORM

Like in the story of Carol's rescue by a human-looking angel with superhuman strength, there are many who have encountered angels who have no wings and look outwardly like any other homo sapiens. This is particularly relevant from the angels- as-aliens perspective being argued for in this book.

For example, Budd Hopkins, considered the premiere researcher of the alien abduction phenomenon, wrote in a book called *Sight Unseen* (coauthored with his former wife, Carol Rainey) about a phenomenon Hopkins called "Normals," human/alien hybrids who appear totally human and yet possess supernatural gifts like telepathy and other forms of mind reading as well as seeming to be "all-knowing" about the real humans they interact with.

What if Hopkins' "Normals" are not hybrids created with alien genetic manipulation but are instead angels?

There is an instance of human-looking angels in the Book of Genesis, specifically the story of Sodom and Gomorrah.

The story begins in Genesis, Chapter 18, with Abraham trying to strike a bargain with the Lord that He spare the two cities if even a small number be righteous among the general population of Sodom and Gomorrah, whose very names have come to be synonymous with degeneracy and perversion. Finally the Lord agrees not to destroy the dens of iniquity if as few as ten righteous are found to dwell therein.

ANGELS OF THE LORD

The first verse of Chapter 19 reads, "The two angels came to Sodom in the evening, and Lot was sitting in the gate of Sodom. When Lot saw them, he rose to meet them, and bowed himself with his face to the earth."

Lot, who is Abraham's nephew, invites the angels to his home to have a meal and rest from their journey before they travel on. After some convincing, the angels agree to accept Lot's hospitality and he makes a feast for them. The angels are obviously human-looking to the extent that they can partake of food and avail themselves of the opportunity to wash their feet.

Before the angels are to lie down for the night, all the men of Sodom, young and old, gather around Lot's home and demand, "Where are the men who came to you tonight? Bring them out to us, that we may know them."

In other words, the men of Sodom wished to have homosexual relations with the angels, taking the angels' human appearance to mean they could engage in sex like mortal men. Lot is shocked by the Sodomites' wickedness, and offers his daughters to the crowd instead rather than risk offending the angels. The Sodomites are angered and try to break down Lot's door and take the angels by force, at which point the angels strike the would-be rapists blind.

The angels warn Lot that they are about to destroy the cities on orders from God and prevail upon Lot to flee along with his family the next morning. The Lord then rains down fire and brimstone on Sodom and Gomorrah, and they are completely wiped out. From a distant vantage point, Lot's uncle Abraham beholds the smoke of the land going up like the smoke of a furnace.

A REPRIEVE FROM THE SHIPS OF HELL

To reiterate, this book is being prepared as an alternative to "the darkness and evil" approach to the nature of the UFOs and their alien occupants. While it is possible to teach the subject either way, one is encouraged by looking to see the angelic as forming at least a portion of the total "big picture" of the UFO phenomenon. A certain sense of "self-preservation" of the soul is called for and one should never feel helpless in the face of "demonic" alien abductions and visitations. When one realizes how enormously complicated the UFO phenomenon is, and also how complicated the moral nature of mankind is, it is readily apparent that none of this is easy to pin down as either good or evil in simple black-and-white terms. Let us go forward with our spiritual searching, and take care that we offend no angels that we meet on our path to salvation. As the material following this introduction explains, we can all have angelic assistance ourselves if we ask for it correctly.

Jacob's Ladder by Angels of the Lord.

Chapter One: Our Guardian Angels

"He hath given his angels charge over thee, to keep thee in all thy ways. In their hands they shall bear thee up, lest thou dash thy foot against a stone. Thou shalt walk upon the asp and the basilisk, and thou shalt trample under foot the lion and the dragon." Psalms 90; 11-13.

Evangelist Billy Graham tells us: "When Christians die, an angel will be there to comfort us, to give us peace and joy even at that most critical hour, and to usher us into the presence of God, where we shall dwell with the Lord forever. Thank God for the ministry of angels."

The Lord promised the protection of an angel for His chosen people during their long and difficult journey to the Promised Land when He said: "Behold I will send my angel, who shall go forth before thee, and keep thee in thy journey, and bring thee into the place that I have prepared."

St. Paul in Hebrews 1:14 says: "Are they not all ministering spirits sent to minister for them, who shall receive the inheritance of salvation?"

The Old Testament does not specify the works of our guardian angels, but even at the time it was written there was a general belief that the saints and the just were protected by an angel or angels.

We also know from reports of those who have passed over into the next life only to be brought back to the living, that they were met by an entity who can only be described as an angel.

Again and again the reports are the same. Take the example of Lillian M., of Milwaukee, Wisconsin, who told her priest: "I don't remember any part of the surgery. But what is vivid in my mind is the great white light I saw. I had a driving urge to walk toward it, but someone stopped me. He was gentle. He told me to go back, that he was not ready for me yet. He said that my place was not ready. He was not dressed in a toga and did not have wings on his back, but he led me to understand without words that he was my guardian angel. I don't know how I knew, I just knew. When I recovered from the surgery I was told that for a minute on the table I was dead."

ANGELS OF THE LORD

The great white light and the entity apparently always appear. Occasionally there are relatives at the entrance into the next life, but among them is always seen the individual who stands ready to ease the newly dead into the next world.

What The Experts Say

One great authority on the subject of angels is F. Suarez, S.J. He tells us: "Even though Scripture does not affirm explicitly the existence of Guardian Angels, nor has the church defined this truth, it is nevertheless universally admitted, and it is so firmly based upon Scripture as interpreted by the Fathers, that its denial would be a very great rashness and practically an error."

Saint Basil the Great says: "That each one of the faithful has an angel who directs his life as a pedagogue and a shepherd, nobody can deny, remembering the words of our Lord: 'See that you despise not one of these little ones.'"

St. John Chrysostom: "Every faithful Christian has an Angel, for every just man had an angel from the very beginning, as Jacob says: 'The angel that nourisheth me and delivereth me from youth.'"

Jesus Himself declares the existence of guardian angels, as you will see when we finish His Father's quote above: "See that you despise not one of these little ones, for I say to you that their angels in heaven always see the face of my Father who is in heaven."

All of the experts agree that Jesus here reveals the wonderful truth that every child has a guardian angel to guide him through life. Theologians take that one step further by saying that adults also have angels who guard them up until the moment of death, then lead them into the Promised Land.

Theologians feel that the guardian angel is given to the child, even though at that stage of the baby's development he receives all of the care and protection he needs from his parents. There are no spiritual dangers to his immortal soul at that point.

But as the child grows he learns to take care of himself. For a greater part of each day he is without the protection of his parents. He is subject to physical and mortal dangers. It makes sense to theologians, therefore, that the guardian angel who watched so carefully over the baby would not abandon the child now that it is out on its own. And as the youth grows he faces more and more dangers and assumes more and more responsibilities. He becomes a parent and must now support a wife and family. His guardian angel, and he surely has one, must now work harder to protect him and guide him.

What We Don't Know About Guardian Angels

There is no information or quote as to the exact moment when a guardian angel assumes his duties with an individual.

We don't know if guardian angels restrict their protection to Christians who are in the state of grace, or if they also guide sinners, pagans, agnostics and atheists. Would an unbaptized baby be privileged with a guardian angel? We don't know.

There is difference of opinion, sometimes from the same writer. For example, the ancient Christian writer Origen made a commentary on Matthew in which he says that all men, faithful or not, have guardian angels. But in his work, **De Principiis**, Origen says: "Each faithful, although the humblest in the church, is said to be attended by an angel who is declared by the Saviour always to behold the face of God the Father, and as this angel was certainly one with the object of his guardianship so, if the latter is rendered unworthy by want of obedience, the Angel of God is said to be taken from him."

St. Jerome says: "Great is the dignity of souls, so great indeed that each of them has an angel assigned for its protection from the moment it is born."

St. Basil and St. Cyril of Alexander felt that only faithful Christian souls have guardian angels, with the former believing that a mortal sin will chase the angel away for good.

St. Thomas said that the guardian angel of a mother carrying a baby might well take care of the unborn infant as well as the mother.

Despite the differences of opinion, theologians today feel that everyone of us has an angel to guide us no matter what our faith is or even if we don't have any faith at all. The angel is with us whether we sin or not. The general opinion is that the angel may not be with us every minute, and that he may even decide not to prevent us from falling into sin or from becoming involved in tribulations. In any case, it should be comforting to know that we are being guarded on a spiritual level by an entity who has our best interests at heart.

How Guardian Angels Protect Us

St. Bernard says that guardian angels surround the souls of the faithful in their charge with plenty of tender love and care. Today we would call it TLC, tender loving care.

They have only one great desire, and that is to lead us through life as safely as possible until we are ready to enjoy the peace that they have in heaven.

Specifically, Guardian Angels:

1. Protect our spiritual and corporal life.
2. Protect and defend us from the seductions of an evil world and the lures of Satan.
3. In many ways they shield us from sudden dangers that threaten our lives. If some harm befalls us they will come to our aid. This point is best illustrated in the protection of little children. How often have you read news stories about children who have been lost in the woods for days, yet survive the ordeal that would kill an older person? And how about children who fall great heights and suffer no physical harm? The guardian angel must take direct action when protecting a child because the child's mind has not yet been developed to the point at which he can comprehend warnings. Adults are different. They can accept or reject a warning. Unfortunately, their rejection often results in unpleasant experiences in spite of the fact that their angelic protector is nearby.
4. One important duty of a guardian angel is the help he must give to his mortal charge in the tremendous work of saving his soul. It is no easy task. His best method is to fill the mortal heart with pious and salutary thoughts of the Supreme Being. The angel also acts as our agent with God, pointing out to God what our fears are and what our needs are. He then returns to us with God's grace and His gifts.
5. Oddly enough, a guardian angel will allow trials and tribulations to come our way so that we may do penance and atone for our faults. An angel may also place violent temptations in our path if only to humble our pride and warn us that we are becoming too complacent.
6. Another vital function is to keep the devil at arms length. This is another task that is not easy, but the attempt is made to reduce temptation, eliminate the possibilities of sin and exclude physical violence and death.
7. Guardian angels pray for us and with us. Our sufferings and our good desires are taken by the angel to God. He battles for our salvation even harder than we do, and perhaps that is because he is more aware of the evil forces which are forever trying to bring us spiritual ruin.
8. One duty is to praise God. They want us to join them in this endeavor. Remember that the Archangel Raphael demanded this

before he would reveal his identity. He said, "Bless ye the God of heaven, give glory to Him in the sight of all that live, because He has shown His mercy to you."

9. Finally, it is in the hour of death that the guardian angel really comes into his own. The soul that he has protected for a lifetime is now committed to his care as he guides it into heaven. At this time, he may ask other angels to give aid if only to make sure the soul is protected from the...

10. Fury of Satan. A clue to the authenticity of this angelic guidance can be found in the words of Our Lord: "And it came to pass, that the beggar died, and was carried by the angels into Abraham's bosom." You can also find this truth in the church's burial service for adults: "May the angels lead thee into Paradise, may the Martyrs receive thee at thy coming, and take thee to Jerusalem the holy city. May the choirs of angels receive thee, and mayest thou with the once poor Lazarus have rest everlasting...Come to his assistance ye Saints of God; meet him the angels of the Lord. Receive his soul and present it to the Most High. May Christ who called thee receive thee, and may the angels lead thee into the bosom of Abraham."

People Who Have Seen Their Guardian Angels

The saintly Padro Pio of Pietrelcinam the stigmatic Capuchin priest who lived at S. Giovanni Rotondo, Italy, not only saw his own guardian angel, but the good angels of many people. Padro Pio often told his followers that if they were in need of spiritual assistance or to ask for prayer, they should send their guardian angels to him. It was reported by an associate that the Padre Pio may have regretted his generosity. At least on one night. He said the following morning that all night long there had been guardian angels arriving with their petitions. He said, "Those guardian angels didn't let me sleep a moment last night."

The church historian Theodoret tells of St. Simeon Stylites who conversed with his guardian angel quite often. The saint lived for 37 years atop a sixty-foot high pillar and was often visibly visited by his angel, who told the saint about the mysteries of God and eternal life. In the end, the guardian angel told him the day on which he would die.

There are also factual accounts of angels joining in with the holy monks in song during the holy hour. St. Benedict reports this in Psalms 137:1. The Venerable Bede confirms St. Benedict's account: "I know that the angels come to the canonical hours and visit our monastic communities; what would they say if they did not find me there among my brethren?"

In one case there was no actual sighting of guardian angels, but their heavenly voices were heard and the aroma of their delicate perfume filled the monastery. This happened in the Monastery of Saint-Riquier. The Abbot Gervin and many of his monks distinctly heard the angels sing and smelled the exquisite perfume.

The founder of the Vallombrosan monks, St. John Gualbert, was actually surrounded by guardian angels as he lay dying. He saw the angels, was aware of their assistance, and heard them sing heavenly praises.

St. Nicholas of Tolentino was permitted to hear his guardian angels and other angels sing every night for the last six months of his life. By the time the end drew near he was anxious to die and be transported to heaven.

St. Francis of Assisi had an singular experience with his guardian angel. The saintly man saw him at the foot of his bed. The angel held a violin and bow. The angel said, "Francis, I will play for you as we play before the throne of God in heaven."

St. Francis said that the angel merely drew the bow across the violin strings just once, and the music was so sweet that all of his cares seemed to vanish. It was as if he was without a body, and that all of his sorrow had melted away.

He told his Brothers the next morning, "And if the angel had drawn the bow across the strings again, then my soul would have left my body from uncontrollable happiness."

Another saint, Frances of Rome, enjoyed many rare privileges. Her guardian angel for 24 years was an archangel. She saw him, heard him, and enjoyed his presence until the day of her death in 1440.

Frances was born of a noble family. She married at the age of 12. She and her husband, Lorenzo Ponziani, had several children. After her husband died in 1436 she joined the Institute of the Oblates, which she founded.

However, many years before that, 1411 to be exact, she suffered a terrible loss. Her son Evangelista was nine years old when he lay dying. Before he drew his final breath he smiled at his mother and said, "Behold the angels who have come to take me to heaven! Mother, I will remember you!"

One year later to the day, St. Frances spent the entire night in prayer. At dawn she saw a brilliant light in the Oratory where she knelt And in that light was her son Evangelista. He wore the same clothes he had on when he died. His lovely features were the same, yet they were more brilliant now. Someone stood beside him, but Frances did not see who it was because she could not tear her eyes from her son.

Evangelista opened his arms to his mother, saying: "I am with the Angels of the second Choir of the first Hierarchy, together with this my young companion, who, as you see, is much more beautiful and resplendent than myself. He is an archangel and in heaven he occupies a place above mine. God sends him to you, dear mother, to be of comfort to you in this life, on your earthly pilgrimage. He will not leave you night or day, and you shall have the sweet satisfaction of seeing him constantly with your bodily eyes. It is God's will that I return to heaven; the sight of this archangel, who will remain with you, shall remind you of me."

Evangelista disappeared. The experience lasted one full hour.

Frances prayed and gave thanks to God for such a glorious gift. She asked the archangel, to help her through her doubts, to give aid during her difficulties, and to keep the devil away from her. Frances found it difficult to look directly at the spiritual being because of the intense brilliance. Her eyes hurt.

Nevertheless, she became aware of the fact that there were times when she was able to look directly at the archangel, and it was then that she saw what looked like a nine-year-old boy, perhaps a little taller. His eyes sparkled and the expression on his face was the loveliest she had ever seen. His white tunic reached to his feet...the tunic over it being similar in color to sky-blue and flaming red. His long hair, which covered his neck and shoulders, was like spun gold. The light from his hair was so bright that Frances often used it to read by at night. She could also go through the dark house at night without a candle, because of the archangel's brilliant hair.

Saint Frances said that when the archangel shook his hair, it was to drive away the approaching devil. She also noticed that her archangel never assumed one position beside her. Sometimes he would be on the right side, then on the left, and even above her. On one occasion, the archangel prevented a suicide from taking place in the Institute of Oblates by holding the individual's knife hand.

During the last four years of her life, Saint Frances was blessed with another Angelic Power who replaced her archangel. He was chosen by God from the myriads of angels in the Angelic Choir of the Powers, and at her death she was visited by this one, plus her archangel, and the guardian angel who had been appointed to her at the time of her birth.

Closer to our own time period (other than Padre Pio who died in 1968), there was Saint Gemma Galgani, who died in 1903.

Although the other cases we mentioned have been authenticated, they are somewhat fragmentary. With St. Gemma there is absolute authentication. If you can find her *Diary, Autobiography, her Letters, or her Life*, written by Fr. Germano di S. Stanislao, C.P., by all means do so. You will find it interesting reading. Besides those documents, there were testimonies from her family and friends.

St. Gemma saw her guardian angel often. They talked. They prayed together. Her angel was a friend. He even stood guard next to her while she slept.

The statements you read here came from her Letters or her Diary.

"Jesus has not left me," she wrote. "He allows my guardian angel to remain with me always."

"This evening after my confession to Father Vallini I felt suddenly agitated and disturbed; it was a sign that the devil was near. The enemy, who had been concealed for some hours, appeared in the form of a tiny little fellow, but so horrible that I was almost overcome with fear. Continuing to pray, all at once I began to experience many blows on my shoulder and this lasted for nearly half an hour. Then my guardian angel came and asked me what was the matter; I begged him to stay all night and he said, 'But I must sleep'. 'No,' I replied, 'the angels of Jesus do not sleep.' 'Nevertheless,' he rejoined, smiling, 'I ought to rest'. Where shall you put me?' I begged him to remain near me. I went to bed; after that he seemed to spread his wings and come over my head. In the morning he was still there."

On June 8, 1899, St. Gemma became a stigmatic. She received five bleeding wounds—her hands, her feet and her side—and her guardian angel was there to assist her. She wrote: "There was pain in my hands and feet and side, and when I got up (from bed), I saw they were dripping blood. I covered them as best as I could and, with the help of my angel, climbed into bed."

The most astounding phenomenon was Gemma's use of her guardian angel to deliver oral messages and letters. Most of the letters went from Lucca to Rome, where Gemma's spiritual director resided. In many cases the reply was delivered by the director's guardian angel. Gemma regarded this astonishing feature as the most natural thing in the world. She wrote on September 15, 1900: "Friday morning I sent a letter through your (the director's) guardian angel. He promised to carry it to you.

"I hope that he took it himself with his own hands. You will let me know at once, won't you?"

Father Germano wrote to Gemma's foster-mother, Signora Cecilia Giannini: "I have received all of the letters sent by Gemma very punctually. I always receive the angelic letters (those brought by angels) faithfully. The fact is unusual, and I confess that I do not understand it at all. I have forbidden her to ask the angel to carry them and he brings them just the same...She (Gemma) ought to ask Jesus and the angel to reassure me with unmistakable signs that would banish every doubt, otherwise, I shall be constrained to forbid absolutely such means of correspondence."

Apparently, Father Germano did receive those signs. After Gemma's death he wrote: "To how many tests didn't I submit this singular phenomenon (of the angel delivering Gemma's letters) in order to convince myself that it took place through a supernatural intervention! And yet none of my tests ever failed; and thus I was convinced again and again that in this, like in many other extraordinary things in her life, heaven was delighted in amusing itself, as it were, with this innocent and dear maiden."

It was during Gemma's stigmata that her guardian angel was most helpful. She wrote to the director: "The blessed angel, on Thursday evening, just before I began to suffer, came again. Together we adored the majesty of God who gave me then such a deep sorrow for my sins that I felt ashamed at finding myself in His presence; I tried to hide myself, to flee. I endured this torment for some time, but the angel then gave me courage...He (the angel) had two beautiful crowns, one of thorns and one of lillies. He asked me which I wished. I wished to obey you, Father, and did not answer at first. Then I said, 'That of Jesus.' He raised the crown of thorns; I kissed it many times, smiling and weeping, and the angel went away."

The angel was such a constant companion to Gemma that she regarded him as one of the family. She was also rather pigheaded with him at times. On many occasions she was heard arguing with her guardian angel in order to get her own way. Father Germano had to remind her that her angel was a blessed spirit and that her proper attitude should be one of trembling.

Gemma was contrite. She said, "You are right, Father. From now on I will show respect and every sign of reverence. I will walk one hundred steps behind him when I see him coming."

Gemma not only had her own guardian angel to see and talk to, she also had others. In particular, there was Father Germano's angel.

He visited Gemma often, especially when her own angel was off somewhere. In one letter to Father Germano she wrote: "Last Friday evening your blessed angel caused me some irritation. I didn't want him around at all, but he said he had so many things to tell me. As soon as he came in he said, 'God bless thee, O'soul entrusted to my care. Of what are you afraid?' I answered, 'Of disobeying.' He said, 'No, it is your spiritual Father who sends me.' Then I let him talk."

When St. Gemma Galgani died in 1903 you can be sure that she went to heaven accompanied by her own guardian angel as well as other angels.

There were scores of holy ones who were able to see their guardian angels with their bodily eyes. There were St. Lidwina of Shiedham, St. Rose of Lima, St. Frances of Rome, St. Gemma, and St. Margaret of Cortona. The latter died in 1297. Margaret had spent her first nine years of life in sin. Her young lover then died a violent death and Margaret resolved to do penance for the rest of her life.

She gave herself to the Franciscan Fathers, offering herself up in prayer, mortification and to the chastising of the flesh.

The Lord saw what she did and forgave her sins. Not only that, He raised her to great sanctity, endowed her with mystical graces, and permitted her to see and hear her guardian angel.

Margaret was overjoyed, yet she could not understand why God would bestow such blessings on a sinner. According to documentation, Margaret cried out to the two apparitions before her. One was her angel, the other was Jesus. She cried, "I have been darkness; I have been darker than the night!"

Christ replied, "For love you, new light, I bless the little cell where you live concealed in My love."

The angel spent most of his time instructing Margaret and reassuring her of God's love. He told her: "God waits for the heart and He makes it careful from the time of love's first desire. When that love demands Him ardently, He no longer defers returning to the soul. Love then achieves in a moment what is accomplished only with time in souls of less ardent charity."

The angel then instructed Margaret on the various degrees of love, namely purgation, illumination and union. He told her: "There are three degrees in this pure love, whereby the faithful and the fervent soul draws her God to herself. When the soul considers herself destitute of all divine love, nothing can comfort her but God. It is then that the Most High inclines and sympathizes with the poor creature who has been given over to anguish...but before the common Father of all goes into the soul that He has created and redeemed, love purifies the heart of all its illusions. The third degree of love is a desire which inflames the spirit like fire. In this final state the soul never ceases to seek her beloved, her spouse, everywhere and in everything."

ANGELS OF THE LORD

Chapter Two: Angels Do Protect Us

It's tragic that movies, books, magazines and television shows continue to hound us with stories about demons, demon possession and Satan worship, yet almost nothing is ever said or written about how angels are with us as invisible good entities to guide us through our tribulations.

Perhaps angel stories don't make for interesting reading, but they do abound. And some of them are quite dramatic.

One such story appeared in the *Reader's Digest* not long ago and told of an experience by Dr. S.W. Mitchell, a well-known neurologist in Philadelphia. He had gone to bed one night bone tired from a long and tiring day. He'd barely gotten to sleep when he was awakened by a knock on his door. Outside was a little girl. She was dressed poorly and was very upset. She begged the doctor to come with her, that her mother was very sick. The night was cold and snowy, but the doctor agreed.

Dr. Mitchell found the woman deathly ill with pneumonia. He immediately arranged for medical care, then complimented the mother for having a daughter who was intelligent and persistent.

The woman gave him a strange look and told him that her daughter had died a month earlier. She said the little girl's clothes were in the closet. The doctor went to the closet and opened it. The thin coat the girl had worn was hanging up. The shoes were on the floor. He touched the coat. It was warm and dry. It had not been out of the house that night.

Had an angel appeared to him disguised as the little girl?

It's quite possible.

Captain Eddie Rickenbacker was convinced that an angel rescued him during World War II. The World War I flying ace was shot down over the Pacific and was lost to the world for weeks on end. His disappearance was reported in newspapers everywhere and thousands of people prayed for him. In fact, Mayor Fiorello LaGuardia asked all of New York City to pray for the fighter pilot.

When Rickenbacker was finally picked up at sea, he wrote an article describing what had happened to him. One section is of particular interest. He wrote:

"And this part I would hesitate to tell, except that there were six witnesses who saw it with me. A gull came out of nowhere, and lighted on my head. I reached up my hand very gently—I killed him and then we divided him equally among us. We ate every bit, even the little bones. Nothing ever tasted so good." Rickenbacker told a listener later that he had no explanation for what happened except that God had sent one of his angels to rescue him.

There are thousands of such stories of how people were rescued by angels. Some stories are actually bone-chilling. Take, for instance, the case of a missionary in the New Hebrides Island whose mission was surrounded one night by hostile natives.

The missionary was The Reverend John G. Paton. He was convinced that the natives intended to burn down the missionary headquarters and then kill him and his wife. The couple spent the entire terror-filled night in deep prayer. In the morning, to their surprise, the natives were gone.

Rev. Paton did not question his good fortune. He did not learn of the reason the natives quit until a year later, when the chief of the tribe converted to Christianity. Paton then reminded the chief about the thwarted attack on the missionary and he asked him why his men decided not to burn it down.

The chief said, 'You had too many men with you, that's why."

Rev. Paton replied, "But there was only my wife and me."

The chief said he was wrong. His men had seen many strong men standing guard, perhaps hundreds of them in shinning garments and long swords in their hands. They circled the missionary and looked so powerful that the natives were afraid to attack.

The Rev. Paton and the chief then agreed that God had sent his angels to protect the missionary and Paton and his wife. The chief was now a believer in Jesus Christ, so he could accept the explanation quite easily.

There is also the tale of the Bible seller in Persia who was stopped by a man who demanded to know if the salesman had a right to sell the Bible in that country.

The seller replied, "We are allowed to sell the Good Book anywhere. Why do you ask?"

The man said, "Because I planned on three different occasions to attack you. But every time I was ready, I saw that you were surrounded by soldiers. So I gave up. Now I no longer wish to do you any harm."

The only logical explanation for that story is that again God sent his emissaries to protect the Bible seller from harm.

The question that begs to be answered now is: How often are we protected by angels without our knowing it?

In the above example the Bible seller was fortunate in learning about his angelic protection. We are probably being protected from bodily harm more often than we realize—only there is no one to tell us about it.

ANGELS OF THE LORD

This is a fact which is frequently expressed in the Bible. If we could only realize that God assures us again and again that His mighty angels are ready to help us in times of stress, there would be little chance of our being attacked by demons. Fortunately, the true Christians today are beginning to understand that there are good forces in the world standing ready and willing to help. These good forces are the ministering angels.

In II Kings 6:14-17 you find an excellent example of angelic power. The King of Syria was anxious to capture the prophet Elisha, who was in Dothan. The king sent his armies there.

Elisha's helper woke up one morning to find the King of Syria's army everywhere on the countryside. He and his master were surrounded. The helper hurried to Elisha to tell him what he saw, and Elisha replied: "Don't be afraid. Our army is bigger than theirs."

The helper thought Elisha had lost his sanity. The prophet then prayed to God to have the young man's eyes opened to see what Elisha saw.

The helper was then able to see a host of angels, horses and chariots of fire on the surrounding hillsides. Elisha was right. His army was far greater than the enemy's.

Paul also had an experience with an angel. You can read it in Acts 27:23-25. He was on a ship headed toward Rome when the ship wrecked. There were 200 crew-members aboard and they thought they were going to drown. Paul spoke to them: "There stood by me this night the angel of God, who I am, and whom I serve, saying, 'Fear not, Paul thou must be brought before Caesar; and lo, God hath given thee all them that sail with thee."

Another striking example of angelic protection occurred in 1942 in Tsingkiangpu, Kiangsu Province, China. The Japanese had won the war with China and were bent now on confiscating all of the stock in all of the Christian Chinese shops.

At one such shop a Japanese truck filled with marines stopped and made ready to do the work. The truck was already half-filled with Christian books, Bibles and religious tracts. Five marines jumped off the truck and started to enter the bookstore. But at that moment a well-dressed Chinese man entered the shop first.

The salesman in the store did not recognize the man, although he did know by name nearly every customer who ever came in. This man though, was a stranger.

Oddly enough, the soldiers did not enter the store. For some strange reason they could not come in. They did loiter around outside. And they did press their noses against the shop's windows to look inside, but they did not enter.

ANGELS OF THE LORD

The soldiers stayed there for fully two hours. The stranger asked the salesman what they wanted, and he was told that the Japanese were confiscating all religious books. The stranger suggested that they pray together until the soldiers left. They did—for two long hours.

Finally, the Japanese climbed back into the truck and drove away.

Soon after that, the stranger left. He bought nothing and did not even ask about any of the items in the store.

The salesman related the story to the shop's owner, and both came to the conclusion that the stranger was really an angel. What is not known is what exactly did the soldiers see when they looked into the store through the windows. It is unfortunate that not one of them was interviewed later. Might we hazard a guess that what was seen was a host of well-armed soldiers standing shoulder-to-shoulder inside the shop?

Noted author Corrie ten Boom captures an unusual experience she had while in the Nazi prison camp called Ravensbruck:

"Together we entered the terrifying building. At a table were women who took away all of our possessions. Everyone had to undress completely and then go to a room where her hair was checked.

"I asked a woman who was busy checking the possessions of the new arrivals if I might use the toilet. She pointed to a door, and I discovered that the convenience was nothing more than a hole in the shower-room floor. Betsy stayed close beside me all the time. Suddenly I had an inspiration. 'Quick, take off your woolen underwear,' I whispered to her. I rolled it up with mine and laid the bundle in a corner with my little Bible. The spot was alive with cockroaches, but I didn't worry about that. I felt wonderfully relieved and happy. 'The Lord is busy answering our prayers, Betsy,' I whispered. 'We shall not have to make the sacrifice of all our clothes.'

"We hurried back to the row of women waiting to be undressed. A little later, after we had our showers and put on our shirts and shabby dresses, I hid the roll of underwear and Bible under my dress. It did bulge out obviously through my dress; but I prayed, 'Lord, cause now thine angels to surround me; and let them not be transparent today, for the guards must not see me,' I felt perfectly at ease. Calmly I passed the guards. Everyone was checked, from the front, the sides, the back. Not a bulge escaped the eyes of the guard. The woman just in front of me had hidden a woolen vest under her dress; it was taken from her. They let me pass, for they did not see me. Betsy, right beside me, was searched.

ANGELS OF THE LORD

"But outside awaited another danger. On each side of the door were women who looked everyone over for a second time. They felt over the body of each one who passed. I knew they would not see me, for the angels were still surrounding me. I was not even surprised when they passed me by; but within me rose the jubilant cry, 'O Lord, if thou dost so answer prayer, I can face even Ravensbruck unafraid.'"

ANGELS OF THE LORD

Chapter Three: An Angel With A Fiery Sword

In this chapter, the late Dr. Frank E. Stranges, who headed the International Evangelism Crusades, Inc., Box 5, Van Nuys, California 91408, tells of his personal encounter with a Guardian Angel.

This is an incident that took place during late November in 1954, while I was on loan to the Secret Service in Boston, Massachusetts. The case involved a group of gentlemen who apparently ran out of money and were actively engaged in the business of printing their own.

Bogus (counterfeit) twenty-dollar bills began to circulate in the tri-State area of New York, New Jersey and Massachusetts. This was cause for a "red alert" because of the coming holiday seasons. It would indeed be a serious matter to contend with, because this was the time of year when money would flow like water in shopping areas throughout the States.

The problem that also worried the authorities was that both the ink and the paper were close to perfect. Only an experienced eye would be able to detect the fact that there was a small impediment in the right eye of President Jackson. It was actually a blur that was not detected by those responsible for proofing the bills before they were printed en masse.

Nevertheless, this would create cause for concern, because very, very few merchants take the time to examine every single twenty dollar bill that is handed to them in a crowded counter.

In other words, it was the plan of the counterfeiters to actually FLOOD the states with bogus twenty dollar bills.

I was working for a Private Investigations Firm at that time, and was requested by my Chief to report to the office without delay. Upon reaching the office, I was greeted by my Chief, John J. Wolf, and was introduced to two United States Secret Service Agents. They then proceeded to inform me that this was an emergency situation, and they were instructed by Washington to retain the services of one whose face was not familiar. At that time, I personally maintained a low profile as the Pastor of the Maranatha Temple, which was an Interdenominational Church.

ANGELS OF THE LORD

My only exposure was at Church three times a week, and every morning over radio station WBMS. My work as a Private Investigator was limited to undercover cases, as well as cases that involved surveillance. In other words, they considered me as one who could perform the required task without being recognized as a resident Federal Agent by those who were engaged in counterfeiting. Night after night, my assignment was to mingle at a special location (a restaurant or bar) and then tail (follow) a certain person who was my target for that particular evening.

There were times when my "subject" drove to Logan International Airport. It was my job to make certain that I carried sufficient cash and passport for any eventuality. This one time, we flew to New York City, where the subject was met at LaGuardia Airport, engaged in a quick board meeting with three other gentlemen in the lounge, and then returned on the next flight back to Boston. It was part of my job to take pictures and include a full description of the gentlemen in question.

I was in the third week of surveillance when the incident in question occurred. My partner, Bill Johnson (who was killed in action two weeks later while on an assignment in Baltimore, Maryland) guarded one end of an alley in back bay Boston. The weather was cold and wet and the wind howled mercilessly from one end of the alley to the other where I was stationed. It seemed that I just could not get warm. I was wearing heavy, fur-lined gloves, and had a heavy scarf wrapped around my head, under which I wore earmuffs.

Then, it started to snow. I was the most miserable of men that terrible black night. The only light was a small naked bulb hanging over a doorway that I was watching. My assignment that night was to stop and question anyone who emerged from that particular door and to hold him until the local police arrived—they would then place him in their vehicle. From then on, I had nothing to do with them.

My partner had similar orders regarding the particular door that he was watching.

Then, in the bitter cold that marked that dark night, all hell cut loose. First, I heard a man scream...over and over again. I turned quickly after tearing off my glove, and grasping for my .38 automatic as I heard, amid the screaming, something heavy and metallic hit the pavement behind me.

I stood ready for anything. Fear tore at my insides as I stood ready...ready for what, I don't know.

Then I heard the footsteps of someone running away from me toward the street to my immediate right. I saw, way off in the distance, the figure of a man who ran, slamming directly into the side of the police car that was a part of our surveillance that fateful night.

I stood trembling for a few moments. My partner shouted to me to ask if I was all right. I said, "Yes, I think so."

He said, "What the hell happened?"

I replied, "Damned if I know."

I hesitated to leave my post until several Federal officers came to the position that I occupied. One of them said to me, "You'd better run out to see what happened."

He relayed the information that a man ran out of the alley, smacked into the side of the police car, and then collapsed. When he came to, he was completely incoherent for the next THREE days.

The fourth day, I was summoned to Police Headquarters, where the "runner" was sitting quietly in a chair with his back to me. One of the Officers said to me, "This is the first day that he even knows his own name. He has a rap sheet longer than your arm. He is also wanted in three states for murder, kidnapping, and anything else you can think of. He also stated over and over again that during the night in question, he raised his .45 level with your head and was about to blow your head off, when he said that he saw a very brilliant light come out of nowhere, and then he claims that he saw a giant Angel-like creature with a large fiery sword in his hand. He said that he was screaming, he dropped his gun, scraped his pants, and ran down the alley away from you."

I slowly approached the "runner," and, as I did, he turned slowly and, when he recognized me, he jumped up from his chair and started to scream uncontrollably. I never placed a hand on him, nor did I ever have an opportunity to speak with him. You see, from that day to this, he has completely lost his mind, and is a resident of a mental institution in the State of New Jersey.

ANGELS OF THE LORD

Chapter Four: Visits With The Angels

Ever since St. Paul saw a vision of Jesus Christ in the desert during his near-death experience, man has had similar visions during those moments when death seemed only moments away.

Usually, we are not so privileged. Nearly all death experiences in which people return are exactly alike. They speak of an extremely intense light, or of a dark tunnel. Friends and relatives long dead appear to them. Sometimes they are shocked to find someone who they did not think of as dead, someone they thought was alive. In many cases the dying person sees the great light and has a compulsion to go to it. In other cases the person is told to go back, that it is not time for him to pass over.

In one recent case a young man in New York City was stabbed and was close to death. Paramedics and doctors worked over him feverishly and miraculously brought him back to the world of the living. The young man then related a strange experience. He said that while he was unconscious he saw his dead brother who had died a year earlier. The brother told him, "Go back! We don't have room for you! Go back!" The young man was aware of hands pushing him away from the area he was in while unconscious. And the area?

Was it Heaven or simply another plane of existence? Even the young man doesn't know. He was aware only of his dead brother, seeing him exactly as he did in life, solid, three dimensional.

No, we all don't see visions of the Holy Family when we are near death. As we said earlier, only a very few are so privileged.

However, there are those who see those benign entities we like to call our guardian angels.

The Lilly Experience

In his autobiography, John Lilly relates a powerful near- death experience. Lilly was best known for his scientific research with dolphins. His book, *"The Center of the Cyclone,"* tells about his meeting with two guardian angels.

He reports that the entities offered him "two sources of radiance, of love, of warmth," and were conveyed to him in a series of "comforting, reverential, awesome thoughts."

Lilly was instructed by the angels in a number of spiritual matters, and he says:

"They say they are my guardian angels, that they have been with me before at critical times and that in fact they are with me always, but I am not usually in a state to perceive them.. .1 am in a state to perceive them when I am close to the death of the body."

Lilly gives some insight into the nature of such guardians in another paragraph:

"Their magnificent deep powerful love overwhelms me to a certain extent, but I finally accept it. As they move closer, I find less and less of me and more and more of them in my being. They stop at a critical distance and say to me that this time I have developed only to the point where I can stand their presence at this particular distance. If they came any closer, they would overwhelm me and I would lose myself as a cognitive entity, merging with them. They further say that I separated them into two, because that is my way of perceiving them, but that in reality they are one in the space in which I found myself. They say that I insist on still being an individual, forcing a projection onto them, as if they were two. They further communicate to me that if I go back to my body as I developed further, I would eventually perceive the oneness of them, and of me, and of many others."

Apparently, Lilly's guardian angels (or angel) had a power that we mortals know nothing about. We can see that they did not want Lilly to get too close to them, or run the risk of being overwhelmed. Yet, the phenomenon is not unique.

The Diotto Experience

Angelo Diotto of Padua, Italy was 10 years old when he nearly drowned in a swimming pool. After his recovery he spoke of his experiences with someone who called himself Angelo's guardian angel.

It was July 10, 1968. Angelo was not an especially religious boy. He avoided going to church whenever possible and was considered quite mischievous. He was devil-may-care and, in fact, it was this lack of fear that had gotten him into trouble in the swimming pool. He had been warned to stay away from the deep end of the pool because he did not know how to swim. But he jumped in, anyway, and nearly drowned.

When lifesavers brought him around, the boy said that he had heard wonderful music in the water, and that when he felt hands pulling him to the surface, he did not want to go.

Angelo told his listeners that after the first few seconds of panic, he did not want to be saved. He said, "I saw things I had never seen before. They were wonderful. A man spoke to me and said he was my guardian angel and that he was always watching over me, but that I made it difficult for him because I was mischievous.

"I wanted to run to him but he held up both hands and told me to stand still. He said I should not get too close to him because I was not ready yet, that I would be returning to the land of the living. He said it was dangerous for me to be too near him.

"Then he started to fade away. Everything became a blur and all of a sudden I was lying on the ground and my mother was crying and men kept pushing some kind of cone on my face."

The Lilly experience concerning the guardian angels' insistence that he not get too close was repeated with Angelo's experience. And it is seen again and again with the near-death experiences of others who have seen and talked to angels who are guardians or guides to the living.

What is this mystical power? No one knows. What we do know is that in every case of near-death in which angels or the Holy Family is involved, there is distance between the subject and the vision. There is always distance between those who have visions in a walking state on earth and the entity being envisioned. In no case on record has anyone seeing a vision been close enough to touch the hem of the garment of the angel, or any member of the Holy Family. Even St. Paul in the desert, when he saw Christ, was not at all close to Jesus.

Children's Visions

Dr. Harold Paul Sloan told incidents of children's deaths. He reported them on a Philadelphia radio station in 1943. In one case there was two-year-old Florence Repp, who lay dying in her grandmother's arms The little girl appeared to be listening to something. Then she said, "Music! Grandma, hear the music?"

The woman replied that she didn't hear anything.

ANGELS OF THE LORD

Little Florence said, "Shush! It's music! They're playing up there!" The girl died seconds later.

Dr. Sloan also told about the two-year-old mongoloid child of Roy Rogers and Dale Evans. On the day of little Robin's funeral the child's nurse told Dale Evans: "Almost all day Sunday, Robin was unconscious, her eyes closed. Well, just a few seconds before she died, she opened her eyes real wide. Then she lifted both her little hands toward the ceiling and smiled radiantly, just as if she knew where she was going and was glad. I've heard of such things happening, Dale, but in all my years of nursing this is the first time I've seen it And I'm sure your baby met our Lord. I saw it happen!"

In another remarkable case, 12-year-old Lowell Jones lost his speech toward the end of his short life on earth. His mother had died years before. Moments before death took him, he raised his arms and cried, "Oh Mother!" It was as though he had found her in the next world.

Famed Washington correspondent Ruth Montgomery told a rather startling story about a six-week-old baby boy who was born with a defective heart. The boy's mother told Montgomery, "Suddenly, our little baby, who was lying in his crib, sat up all by himself and looked straight at me. I was terribly shaken, not only because I had never heard of so young a baby raising and holding himself erect, but because of the unfathomable look in his big blue eyes. It was an other-world gaze, wise, adult, which plainly told me that he was not going to live, and that I was not to grieve."

Visions During Great Disasters

There are hundreds of stories of out of body experiences in which the dying later tell of seeing their own bodies on operating tables, or on floors while people work feverishly over them to bring life back. The dying tell us of their visions of the Holy Family, of angels, of Christ on the cross. However, it has also been shown that visions can occur to those who are threatened with disaster—especially when great masses of people are threatened by the same disaster.

For instance, in April 1944, Englanders daily faced annihilation from Hitler's Luftwaffe. They had lived under the Nazis' bombs for five years and there seemed no end of it.

On April 27 in Ipswich, during an air raid, hundreds of people saw a vision in the sky It was Christ on the Cross. London newspapers carried the story and on May 7, the Chicago Tribune Press Service sent a dispatch which read in part:

"...numerous residents of eastern England stoutly maintain that the sign of the cross was visible in the sky for fifteen minutes. Those who have given detailed descriptions include a naval commander, a carpenter, housewives, etc. The consensus of the statements is that the vision gradually grew clearer until the figure of Christ was distinct. The local pastor is investigating..."

One eyewitness was William Garnham, an engineer. He said: "I saw the sign of the cross actually form. There was no mistake in either the shape of the crucifix or the figure nailed to it." The cross was surrounded by visions.

On May 8 the local pastor, Rev. Harold Godfrey Green, vicar of St. Nicholas Church and army chaplain, reported that he had interviewed 2,000 eyewitnesses. His conclusion was: "There was scarcely any variation—if any—in these accounts. I have verified the fact of the vision quite definitely. I am satisfied myself beyond doubt of the authenticity of the vision.

"There were clouds in the sky which drifted by while the vision remained stationary!"

History abounds in such cases. You can find numerous accounts of spiritual help coming to people in times of trouble. The Crusaders were sure they saw angelic hosts fighting for them on several occasions—and the phantom horsemen came at a time when the Crusaders were certain they were about to be destroyed.

In the wars between the English and Scots, several cases of divine intervention were cited, and again during the Napoleonic wars. The most famous of all sightings, however, occurred during the latter part of August, 1914, over France.

So much first-hand and sincere testimony has been given that we can scarcely doubt the event. The occurrences were titled "The Angels of Mons." Again, one force of soldiers was threatened with annihilation by another. The British Army had 80,000 men in the field of Agincourt. They were opposed by 300,000 Germans who were backed up by terrific artillery fire.

During that period the Allies' dream of an early victory had been wiped out by the endlessly advancing Germans. But quite suddenly all of that was to change.

An eyewitness named Lance Corporal Headley-Johns of the Lancashire Fusiliers reported later: "I was with my battalion in the retreat from Mons on or about August 28. It was between eight and nine in the evening. I could see quite plainly in mid-air a strange light which seemed to be quite distinctly outlined and was not a reflection of the moon, nor were any clouds in the neighborhood.

"The light became brighter and I could see quite distinctly three shapes, one in the center having what looked like spread wings. The other two were not so large but quite plainly distinct from the center one. They appeared to have a long loose hanging garment of gold tint, and they were above the German lines and facing us.

"We stood watching them for about three quarters of an hour. All the men with me saw them, and other men came up from other groups who also told us they'd seen the same thing."

On the same night, August 28, 1914, a wounded RAF man told nurse Phyllis Campbell: "We all saw it. First there was a yellowish mist sort of rising before the Germans as they came to the top of the hill. I just gave up. No use fighting the whole German race. The next minute, comes this funny cloud of light, and when it clears off there's a tall man with yellow hair and golden armor on a white horse, holding his sword up. Before you could take a breath, the Germans had turned and we were after them."

Captain Cecil Wightmick Haywood of the first corps British Intelligence witnessed the rout of the Germans. He said that the Germans fled in panic and confusion, dropping their weapons and supplies and running like mad toward their homeland.

Captain Haywood learned later that the Germans had been shelling British machine gun nests when they suddenly shifted their fire to a deserted area. One British sergeant said in amazement, "Fritz has gone balmy. Why is he preparing that open ground?"

That, too, was explained when Captain Haywood interrogated German prisoners. One said: "They were all clad in white. Mounted on white horses. We all saw them. We turned our big weapons and our machine gun on them, but they kept coming. The concentration of fire power was tremendous, but not a single white horseman fell."

The intervention of the "Angels of Mons" turned the tide of battle. The Allied position was no longer desperate.

Chapter Five: Our Link With Angels

Martin Luther: An angel is a spiritual creature without a body created by god for the service of Christendom and the church.

It is unfortunate but true—the devil has little trouble getting his name mentioned almost everywhere, yet we rarely hear anything (or read anything) about angels. The devil and his demons fill entire bookshelves with volume after volume about their evils. Motion picture companies turn out scores of movies about Satan's works. But when was the last time you read a book or saw a movie about angels?

From a practical standpoint, of course, the devil makes better copy. And if you were to believe all the books and movies about him you would assume that the link between the devil and mortal man is powerful, so powerful in fact that angels don't stand a chance of getting our attention.

Actually, quite the reverse is true. We are linked much more closely with angels. They are with us all the time, and are especially attentive to us in times of strife. It is said that when we pass over, the first to greet us on the other side is an angel who helps us make the transition. We are comforted by the entity. We are assured that our new life will be a good one, that we have nothing to fear.

On earth, our angels are forever near, guiding us to the right path. In nearly every instance we are not aware of their help and we never acknowledge them. Yet they continue to work for us without recognition, without applause, without even our thanks.

Take the case of the New York City woman who was destitute. She had ten dollars left to her name and had a small baby to feed. Her husband deserted her. She lost her job. Her unemployment insurance ran out. She owed rent money. Her utilities were about to be shut off. She intended to spend her last ten dollars for baby food and have nothing to eat for herself.

The woman had been advised to accept welfare, but she could not bring herself to do it. She had worked all of her life. She had never been out of work until now. But she had to be practical. She despised the idea of accepting a hand-out, yet there was no other way.

She picked up her phone and dialed the number of the local welfare office. But the person who answered said, "IBM, good morning."

She had dialed the wrong number. The woman from IBM heard a tearful woman, a stranger, say that she was destitute. The two of them began to talk. Soon the desperate woman broke down. The IBM woman took action. She spoke to someone at the office, then returned to the caller, saying that a job opening had taken place and that she should come in right away.

The woman did so and is now an executive with the firm.

Question: Did she dial the wrong number by accident, or did an angel guide her finger? We like to think an angel was responsible for her good fortune. In the woman's time of strife an angel came to her rescue.

If you read Adela Rogers St. John's book, "***Tell No Man***," you will find an amazing account of angels doing battle with enemy in the skies during World War II. The story was not revealed until a few months after the war was over. It came to light during a celebration dinner held in honor of Air Chief Marshall Lord Hugh Dowding.

It was an important occasion. The Royal Air Force with no help from anyone had managed to save Great Britain from invasion and defeat during those early years of the war. Now the feast was held to honor the man who had done so much for his country— Lord Hugh Dowding. The King and the Prime Minister were there, along with other dignitaries.

When it came time for Lord Dowding to speak, he praised his men to the skies for their spirit. He said the compliment was small. His men rarely slept. They seemed always to be in the air, flying to meet the enemy.

And he told about a mission in which his airmen had been killed or seriously wounded, yet their planes kept flying and fighting. He said that on many occasions there seemed to be no logical reason why the planes should still be in the air, yet they were, and were still functioning as fighting machines. Pilots who landed safely later reported seeing figures in the cockpits still operating the controls even though the pilots were dead.

Lord Dowding was convinced that the planes were operated by angels.

Naturally, there is no way to prove it, but certainly someone was flying those planes.

War is a period of extreme strife, and apparently angels are ready to be of assistance to man in such times. During the Korean

ANGELS OF THE LORD

War it was evident that angels were on hand when a small group of American Marines from the First Division were in real trouble.

They were in enemy territory. The temperature was 20 degrees below freezing and the men had no shelter. There was a good chance that all would be frozen to death. And if that didn't happen then they would starve to death because they hadn't eaten in six days.

The group was ready to surrender to the Chinese. They had no alternative. At least, they would be fed and housed.

One of them, however, recited several verses from Scripture. He pleaded with the men to sing a song praising God. They did so. But the song was barely finished when they heard a terrific crashing sound. They turned in time to see a wild boar charging them.

The squad jumped out of its way, but the animal stopped suddenly. One soldier raised his rifle to shoot him, but it wasn't necessary. The boar keeled over, dead. That night the soldiers had a fine meal of cooked boar.

When they went to sleep that night they felt better, but it was still miserably cold. The next morning they heard a noise in the distance and felt sure that their time had come, that the Chinese were about to capture them.

That wasn't the case. The noise they heard was made by a South Korean who knew how to speak English. The man said to the soldiers, "I will show you out."

He led them through trails winding around mountains and finally deposited them behind their own lines. And when the soldiers turned to thank the South Korean, he was gone. He had completely vanished.

Mortal man...or angel? So you see, there does appear to be a strong link between man and the angels. It is also obvious, however, that the angels are at their best during times of strife, when man is sorely in need of divine help. An angel, even your own guardian angel, can't be expected to jump to your aid every time you have a minor problem. Let it suffice that he watches over you. Be assured that he is there when you really need him.

How Many Angels?

Of course, no one can know the answer to that question. The Bible mentions angels nearly 300 times, but only two are mentioned by name. Gabriel appeared three times. Daniel saw Gabriel in a dream.

Zacharias saw him while he was working and learned that his wife would give him a son, who was John the Baptist. He also appeared before the Virgin Mary in Nazareth.

Michael is the second angel. You will remember that Michael fought the devil over the body of Moses. He formed an alliance of angels to fight a dragon in heaven.

There is, of course, a third angel—Lucifer. He is known as the fallen angel. "How art thou fallen from heaven, O Lucifer, son of the morning! How art thou cut to the ground, which didst weaken the nations!" Isaiah 14:12.

What we do know is that the number of angels remains constant. Obedient angels don't die. Scholars tell us that when Lucifer found it necessary to rebel against God, he took one-third of all of the angels with him. The Book of Hebrews describes the number of angels, good and bad, as innumerable company. That could mean that the host is so vast that it would stagger our imaginations. Purely as a guess, scholars feel that the one-third who went with Lucifer numbers in the hundreds of thousands. And it is frightening to think that these angels are now demons.

Do Angels Eat?

We already know that angels are not the same as men. They are celibate, and they don't procreate. However, there is plenty of evidence to substantiate the theory that angels do eat when they are in human form. The Bible doesn't say anything about the need of angels to eat to stay alive, yet it recounts instances of them enjoying food and drink.

For example, there is the bread of angels, which David referred to when the children of Israel were given manna to eat in the wilderness. Look at Psalm 78:25 and you will find Asaph saying: "Man did eat angels' food." Elijah did eat angels' food which kept him going for forty days and forty nights. Remember the Biblical story? Elijah won a great victory over the priests of Baal on Mount Carmel. The great prophet was tired and discouraged, especially because Jezebel now threatened his life. Elijah was at an extremely low point in his life despite his victory. So God's angel appeared before him and set out a wonderful spread of good things to eat and drink. Elijah ate twice, and was so fortified that he was able to sustain himself the time period mentioned above. (I Kings 19:5).

Take a look at Genesis 18:1, 2. Here you will find three angels eating with Abraham. One of these angels may well have been Jesus Christ. In any event, Abraham was camped in the plains of Mature when he received his divine visitation, and Abraham supplied all of the food and drink.

And in Genesis 19 you will find the destruction of Sodom and Gomorrah. Here, two angels came to save Lot and his family. Lot made a feast and the angels joined in, even eating unleavened bread.

How Smart Are Angels?

They are more knowledgeable than man, but they don't know everything. Undoubtedly, they know more about us than we know about ourselves, but you can rest easy that they will never use their knowledge to hurt us. Angels are actually ministering spirits. Anything they know about us will be used for our good.

If you read Mark 13:32 you will find out that angels are not omniscient. Here you learn that Jesus said of His Second Coming: "But of that day and that hour knoweth no man, no, not the angels which are in heaven."

And in II Samuel 14:20 you will see the story of Job who asks a woman of Tekoah to talk to King Solomon about urging him to bring Absalom back to Jerusalem. Her reply was, "My lord is wise, according to the wisdom of an angel of God, to know all things that are in the earth."

Angels are not like God. Their knowledge is vast, but there is a limit to it. Nevertheless, in this day and age, in which men are unable to keep anything secret for very long, it is assuring to know that angels will never use what they know about us for evil purposes.

Are Angels "All Powerful"?

They certainly are not all powerful, but they do possess an amazing strength, as is pointed out in II Thessalonians when Paul refers to them as the "mighty angels of God." In II Peter 2:11 we see that "angels who are greater in might and power (than man) do not bring a reviling judgment against them before the Lord." And David tells us in Psalm 103:20 that "angels exceed in strength."

God used angels to scatter the people of Israel because of their sins. He also used them during the trying period of Sodom and Gomorrah. These two cities were given over to wickedness to such a degree that God judged them and decreed that they had to be destroyed.

He did not destroy them without warning. He sent angels to Abraham, who told him that the two cities were facing an approaching doom. Abraham's nephew was Lot and Lot and his family lived among the wickedness. Abraham did not want to lose his nephew in the great destruction, so he pleaded with God to spare the two cities.

Abraham's strong arguing point was that if he found fifty righteous people living in Sodom he would hope that God would spare the city. God agreed. But Abraham could not find fifty righteous people so he asked God if He would settle for 45 such people. Again God agreed. But Abraham was in a bind. There weren't 45 righteous people in Sodom. He asked God if He would avert His terrible judgment if he found 30 righteous people. God said He would. Abraham tried again, then asked God for 20 people, then 10. God said He would withhold judgment if Abraham came up with 10 people who were not wicked in Sodom. But Abraham failed to find them.

Exasperated with Abraham's nonsense, God put the wheels of destruction into motion. He sent two angels to warn Lot and his family to get out of Sodom immediately. While the angels were in Sodom, the wicked people had the audacity to try to molest the heavenly messengers. The angels promptly blinded them.

As soon as Lot and his family were beyond the city limits, God did not personally destroy Sodom and Gomorrah, but sent His ministers of judgment (angels) to do the job. The two cities and all of the people in them were destroyed.

You can get some idea of the power of a single angel by reading II Kings 19. The Assyrian army was camped outside Jerusalem—185,000 soldiers. The city certainly appeared to be doomed. In fact, the commander sent a letter to King Hezekiah and it was obvious what the commander wanted.

King Hezekiah turned to God for help. The answer God gave him was that not a single Assyrian arrow would be fired on Jerusalem. This, He said, was a promise to David that He would defend the city. And He did. One angel was sent to the field of battle during the night. The following morning the entire Assyrian army lay dead.

But there did come a time when David defied God's command by numbering Israel. In reply, God sent a pestilence so powerful that 70,000 Israelites were killed. He then sent one angel to destroy the city. David saw the angel of the Lord stand between the earth and the heaven, having a drawn sword in his hand stretched out over Jerusalem (I Chronicles 21:16).

Looking at this awesome sight, David's only hope was to beg for mercy. There was simply no way he or anyone could avert a terrible tragedy.

David did plead for mercy. The New Testament tells us that avenging angels have judged the unrighteous acts of men and nations, but in this case the angel told David to set up an altar. He suggested that it be done on the threshing floor of Oman the Jebusite.

David obeyed, and when God accepted David's sacrifice on the altar He told the angel, "It is enough; stay now thine hand" (Samuel 24:16).

In the case of Herod Agrippa, we see an angel smiting him because Herod thought he was God. In modern day parlance it could be said that Herod believed his own press.

The Name Elohim

It was understandable in the beginning that man would look upon angels as divine beings. After all, the angels were splendid, wise, beautiful and powerful. What's more, they were spiritual. In the Old Testament you will find that one of the names given to angels in Elohim. This is the same name that was given to God. It also meant Godlike beings—and false gods.

The name eLohim is found in the Book of Psalms: "Let them be all confounded that adore graven things, and that glory in their idols. Adore Him, all you His Angels." (eLohim—the gods). Also in Psalms: "I will sing praise to thee in the sight of the angels." (eLohim—the gods). The fact that angels are called gods is meant to be taken in the context that saints and prophets are also called gods.

"Sons of God" or Beney Elohim

This name and the one before it, Elohim, is applied to angels and to men who are just. Angels and just men are drawn into one family through the element of sanctifying grace. They are all of God's family, making them children of the same Father. Angels and saints are sons of God, and therefore brethren.

ANGELS OF THE LORD

"Messenger" or Maleakh

This word actually explains what angels really are—messengers of God. This is their best known duty. Angels are called upon more frequently to act as messengers than anything else. The name MALEAKH refers to all the heavenly spirits of any rank or Choir, and it is also the proper name of the spirits of the last Choir in the last Hierarchy.

"Mediators" or Melis

The title is descriptive rather than nominal. You can read it only in the Old Testament. Look in the Book of Job 33:23 and you will read: "If there shall be an angel (a mediator) speaking for him, one among thousands, to declare a man's uprightness."

All good angels and especially our guardian angels are our mediators. They speak for us before God. The angel Raphael was Tobias' mediator when he said: "When thou didst pray with tears, and didst bury the dead, and didst leave thy dinner, and hide the dead by day in thy house, and bury them at night, I offered thy prayer to the Lord."

The idea of angelic mediation is expressed in the sacred liturgy of the Mass: "We humbly beseech Thee, Almighty God, bid these our offerings to be brought by the hands of Thy holy angel.

It happened when he appeared before his people to make a speech. He was dressed elegantly in his royal garb. Apparently, his eloquence was such that when he finished speaking, the people shouted to him: "It is the voice of a god and not of a man."

Herod was overjoyed. God was not "because he gave not God the glory." And in Acts 12:23 we read that "The angel of the Lord smote him."

"When I See the Blood, I Will Pass Over You."

How terrifying it must have been for the Egyptians and Israelites that awesome midnight, just before the Exodus when a destroying angel came down from heaven to kill the first born of every unbelieving Egyptian and Israelite.

This heart-rending account has been the theme of Christians and Jews for centuries. You can read about it in Exodus 12:18-30. The gist of the story is that Jews who believed in God offered sacrifices to Him and then sprinkled the doorposts and lintels of their homes with the blood. His minister of judgment (the destroying angel) descended (1 Corinthians 10:10, Hebrews 11:28), and took the first born of every household in which there were unbelievers.

"When I see the blood, I will pass over you," has been the text of Rabbis and Christian clergymen in thousands of sermons.

It was the faith of those living in the blood-sprinkled houses that really counted with God.

More to the point for our purposes, the story demonstrates the awesome power of an angel.

Abraham, Isaac and The "Angel"

Abraham heard those shattering words from God: "Abraham... take now thy son, thine only son Isaac, whom thou lovest, and get thee into the land of Moriah; and offer him there for a burnt offering upon one of the mountains which I will tell thee of." (Genesis 22:1-2)

God's words were plain. He wanted Abraham to kill his only son, Isaac. You can easily understand the torment Abraham experienced that long night when he contemplated the horror of such an act. Yet, Abraham knew perfectly well that God was testing his faith. He could not disobey.

In the morning, Abraham collected wood for a fire with his son and set out for the land of Moriah. On a mountaintop he prepared the altar. His heart ached him when he tied Isaac's hands and feet.

He unsheathed his knife. His eyes looked to the sky. He raised the blade to the heavens, ready now to do God's will.

Then suddenly, as we are told in Genesis 22:11-12, "The angel of the Lord called unto him out of heaven, and said, Abraham, Abraham...Lay not thine hand upon the lad, neither do thou anything unto him; for now I know that thou nearest God, seeing thou hast not withheld thy son, thine only son from me."

Of course, Abraham responded immediately. His sorrow was lifted. The relief he felt was enormous. And for his unqualified obedience, God rewarded him with a live goat which could be used as a burnt offering. The goat appeared nearby, his horns locked into a thicket. Abraham took the animal and offered him up for the burnt offering instead of his son.

The key word here is "instead." It will be explained in a moment. The point now, however, is whether an angel appeared before Abraham or whether it was Jesus Christ in the guise of an angel.

There are Biblical scholars who believe the latter. This is called a "theophany," or the appearance of God to man.

God was trying to make a very important point here. We ask ourselves could it be possible that God would ask for a human sacrifice? Is He so cruel as to demand that a man kill his own son as a burnt offering?

Before you reply, consider that God Himself was ready to sacrifice His own Son. Jesus Christ died "instead" of all of us who believe in Him. God did not ask Abraham to do anything He was not ready to do Himself. In Romans 8:32 you see, "He that spared not His own Son, but delivered Him up for us all, how shall He not with Him also freely give us all things?"

It is clear that God's emissaries are forever ready to carry out His judgment against those of us who deliberately reject Jesus Christ and God's salvation. We are not talking about those of us who are sinners because all of us are sinners by nature and often by choice. The fierce judgment of God comes not to the sinners but to those who insist on rejecting His Son.

Chapter Six: Organization of Angels

Although some see the organization of angels as conjecture, there does seem to be a pattern among them consisting of nine levels in terms of authority and glory.

They are archangels, angels, seraphim, cherubim, principalities, authorities, powers, thrones and finally might and dominion. For verification, check Colossians 1:16 or Romans 8:37. The groupings actually were divided by the Medieval theologians.

And you can find experts who feel that some of these groupings, for instance the principalities, authorities and thrones, might actually be human institutions and human beings.

Matthew Henry quotes Paul in Colossians when Henry says that Christ "made all things out of nothing, the highest angel in heaven as well as men upon the earth. He made the world, the upper and lower world, with all the inhabitants of both...He (Paul) speaks here as if there were several orders of angels: 'Whether thrones, or dominions of principalities or powers,' which must signify either different degrees of excellence or different offices and employments."

Archangel

The prefix "arch" suggests a chief or a great angel. The Bible tells us that there is only one archangel, and that is Michael. Lucifer undoubtedly was an archangel until he fell from grace. We don't know if he was equal to or above Michael before his fall.

In the Old Testament, Michael figures prominently in connection with Israel as a nation. God speaks of Michael as the prince of His chosen people—"the great prince which standeth for the children of Thy people." Daniel 12:1. However, it must be understood that Michael protects and defends all people, no matter who they are.

Revelation 12:7-12 tells us that it is Michael who will lead the armies that will do battle with Satan, the great dragon, and all of his demons. This will be the last titanic conflict of the age. Michael will be victorious. Hell will tremble. There will be rejoicing in heaven.

Experts of the Bible say that Michael is the one who cast out Satan and his angels from heaven, and that even today the archangel is in constant battle with Lucifer.

Michael the Archangel will be with Christ at the Second Coming. You can read that in 1 Thessalonians 4:16, in which it is said: "For the Lord Himself shall descend from heaven with a shout, with the voice of the archangel... and the dead in Christ shall rise first."

Gabriel, God's Messenger

In Hebrew, "Gabriel" means "God's hero." Also, "The Mighty One." It can also be interpreted to mean "God is great." Gabriel is usually referred to in the Scriptures as "the messenger of Jehovah" or "the Lord's messenger." Oddly enough, although the Bible never refers to Gabriel as an archangel, it does mention him more often than it does Michael.

Gabriel is the bearer of good news in the Bible and he appears four times. The angel makes his first appearance in Daniel 8:15, 16, when he announces the vision of God for the "end time." Gabriel has been charged by God to convey the message that reveals God's plan in history. Gabriel says in verse 17 of the Amplified Bible that we are to "understand...the vision belongs to (events that shall occur in) the time of the end."

Daniel says: "While I was speaking in prayer, the man Gabriel, whom I had seen in the former vision, being caused to fly swiftly, came near to me and touched me about the time of the evening sacrifice."

Gabriel then revealed the awesome sequence of events which would occur at the "end time," or at the time when all history would culminate in the return of Christ.

Gabriel also appears in Luke 1, the New Testament, when he identifies himself to Zacharias, announces the birth of John the Baptist, and describes his life and ministry as the forerunner of Jesus.

An even more important appearance is made by Gabriel when he appears before the Virgin Mary to tell her of Jesus. He told Mary:

"Fear not, Mary, for thou hast found favor with God. And, behold, thou shalt conceive in thy womb, and bring forth a son, and shalt call his name Jesus...And he shall reign over the house of Jacob forever, and of his kingdom there shall be no end (Luke 1:30-33)."

ANGELS OF THE LORD

Seraphim

In Hebrew, seraph means "to burn." Seraphim is the plural of seraph. You will find it only twice in the Sacred Scripture. In Isaiah 6:1: "I saw the Lord sitting upon a throne high and elevated, and his train filled the temple. Upon it stood the seraphims: the one had six wings, and the other had six wings; with two they covered his face, with two they covered his feet, and with two they flew."

Also in Isaiah we find the seraphim purging with fire: "One of the seraphims flew to me: and in his hand was a live coal, which he had taken with the tongs off the altar. And he touched my mouth, and said: 'Behold this hath touched thy lips, and thy iniquities shall be taken away, and thy sin shall be cleansed.'"

The Bible really does not support the common belief that angels have wings. The idea got its start when it was assumed that angels had wings because of their ability to move from place to place in an incredibly short time. Still, Isaiah does say that the seraphims had six wings.

Nevertheless, the seraphims are "the Burning Ones." Their first duty is to sing without stopping in the presence of God. The seraphic hymn of glory that was heard by the Prophet was: Holy, holy, holy, the Lord God of hosts, all the earth is full of His glory."

The seraphim never show their faces, according to the experts on the subject. No one knows what the facial features might be, and it is also assumed that the body might be human in appearance, yet there is no documentation on this, either.

Cherubim

Cherubim are the heavenly protectors of holy places and holy things. In Genesis 3:23 you find that cherubim are the first to be mentioned in the category of angels: "And the Lord God... placed before the paradise of pleasure cherubims, and a flaming sword, turning every way, to keep the way of the tree of life."

The Lord commanded Moses to make the images of two Cherubim in the Tabernacle, thereby representing them as guardians of holy places and holy things. The Lord said: "Thou shalt make also two cherubims of beaten gold, on the two sides of the oracle. Let one cherubim be on the one side, and the other on the other. Let them cover both sides of propitiatory wherewith the ark is to be covered."

Dionysius described the cherubim aptly: "The name cherubim denotes their power of knowing and beholding God, their receptivity to the most high gift of light, their contemplation of the beauty of the Divinity in its first manifestation. They are filled by participation in divine wisdom, and bounteously outpour to those below them from their own fountain of wisdom."

What do cherubims look like? According to Ezekiel, "Each one had four faces, and each one had four wings, and the likeness of a man's hand was under their wings."

The Thrones

This Angelic Choir is rather mysterious in the Scriptures. We don't know much about their duties. We find them at the head of a partial list in Col. 1:16, in which it is said: "In him (the word) were all things created in heaven and on earth, visible and invisible, whether thrones or dominations, or principalities or powers."

With the seraphim and the cherubim, the thrones enjoy the glory of being closer to the throne of God than all the others in the Angelic Choirs. Since they are near to God, the light of the divine mysteries is brought to them first. Dionysius: "The name of the most glorious and most exalted thrones denotes that which is exempt from the untainted by any base and earthly thing...They have no part in what is low but dwell in the fullest power, immovable and perfectly established in the Most High."

The Dominations

We must turn to Dionysius again for enlightenment on the Dominations: "The name given to the holy Dominations means, I think, a certain unbounded elevation to that which is above, freedom from all that is terrestrial, and from all inward inclination to the bondage of discord, a liberal superiority to harsh tyranny, freedom from degrading servility and from what is low, because they are untouched by any inconsistency. They are true lords, perpetually aspiring to true lordship and to the source of all lordship...They do not turn towards vain shadows, but wholly give themselves to that true authority, forever one with the Godlike source of lordship."

Dionysius tells us that the Dominations occupy the first place in the second Angelic Hierarchy.

The Virtues

We find the Virtues mentioned by St. Peter when he refers to good angels: "Angels, Powers and Virtues." St. Paul mentions quite a few when he says: "All Principality, and Powers, and Virtue, and Dominion," saying so in the sense that they are good spirits. However, a sour note creeps in when the Apostle Paul talks about the Virtues being hostile to Christ, that is, among the fallen angels. He says, "When He (Christ) shall have brought to nought all principality, and power, and virtue."

Again we must turn to Dionysius for a better description of the Virtues: "The name of the holy Virtues signifies a certain powerful and unshakable courage welling forth into all their Godlike energies...mounting upwards in fullness of power to an assimilation with God, never falling away from the divine life through its own weakness, but ascending unwaveringly to the super-essential Virtue which is the source of all virtue, fashioning itself as far as it may in virtue.. .and flowing forth providentially to those below, filling them abundantly with virtue."

The Powers

It is generally assumed that the Holy Powers form the third and last Choir of the second Angelic Hierarchy. In the Old Testament, in Daniel, we read: "O, all ye powers of the Lord, bless the Lord." In the New Testament you will find in Eph. 3:10 "That the manifold wisdom of God may be made known to the Principalities and the Powers in heavenly places through the church."

Again, Dionysius tells us: "The name of the Holy Powers, co-equal with the Domination and Virtues, signifies an orderly and unconfined order in the divine receptions, and the regulation of intellectual and supernatural power which never debases its authority by tyrannical force but is irresistibly urged on in due order to the divine. It beneficiently leads those below it, as far as possible to the Supreme Power which is the source of power."

The Angels

The angels are the real link with man. They are the lowest Choir of all of the Hierarchies and are the last of the heavenly beings possessing angelic nature. The word angel means messenger, and their Choir is more directly in contact with visible and earthly things.

ANGELS OF THE LORD

How Angels Are Ranked

THE SUPREME HIERARCHY
Seraphim, Cherubim and Thrones

MIDDLE HIERARCHY
Dominations, Virtues, Powers

LOWER HIERARCHY
Principalities, Archangels, Angels

The Language of Angels

We know beyond doubt that angels have their own language when they converse with each other. We don't know what that language is. What we do know is that when angels appear before men, human language is spoken.

St. Thomas feels that angels talk to each other by means of illumination, which is nothing more than the conveyance of thoughts and ideas by opening their minds. No speech is necessary.

St. John says: "They (the angels) need neither tongue nor ears but without the help of any spoken word they exchange with each other their thoughts and their counsels."

The language of the angels, therefore, is much clearer, stronger and more perfect than the spoken language of men. Understand, our spoken words are merely the symbols of our ideas and thoughts. Sometimes these symbols are inadequate for full expression. We don't often get the full meaning, nor are we often very clear to our listener.

How Angels Get About

An angel is spiritual and immaterial. He does not occupy space, not even a single point—which brings up the inanity about how many angels can dance on the head of a pin. The question is silly, to say the least.

Another thing—an angel can be engaged in only one place at a time. He can, however, make himself known by the application of his power. If you read John 5:4 you will see the well-known account of the miraculous cures that took place in the pond called Bethsaida by the Sheepgate of Jerusalem. "An Angel of the Lord descended at certain times into the pond and the water was moved. And he that went down first into the pond after the motion of the water was made whole, of whatsoever infirmity he lay under."

We don't know by this account that anyone saw the angel, but we do learn that an angel can affect material objects just the way a soul or demons can.

An angel can pass from one place to another with the speed of thought, but he can't be in two places at once. He can do in reality what we can do only mentally. We can picture ourselves in some far-off land, but angels can actually be there simply by thinking he is there.

The Bible tells us that angels have transported material objects and people with the same rapidity they enjoy at all times.

Though most angels are depicted with wings, in actuality they can often appear as strangers willing to assist in many of life's problems.

Remember Daniel in the lion's den? This is a good example of an angel transporting a human being over a great distance.

The Prophet Daniel was in the lion's den for six days. The Lord sent an angel to fetch food for Daniel. Was the angel's task to get some real food for Daniel, who, incidentally, was not touched by the hungry felines.

Daniel was in Babylon. The angel went to Judea, which was 600 miles west of Babylon. In Daniel 14:32-38 we read: "There was in Judea a prophet called Habacuc, and he boiled pottage, and had broken bread in a bowl, and was going into the field, to carry it to the reapers. And the Angel of the Lord said to Habacuc: Carry the dinner which thou hast into Babylon to Daniel, who is in the lions' den. And Habacuc said: Lord, I never saw Babylon, nor do I know the den. And the angel of the Lord took him by the top of his head, and carried him by the hair of the head, and set him in Babylon over the den in the force of his spirit. And Habacuc cried saying: Daniel, thou servant of God, take the dinner that God hath sent thee...And Daniel rose and ate. And the Angel of the Lord presently set Habacuc again in his own place."

We can assume that all of this took place in a moment of time, so that Habacuc was able to prepare another meal for his reapers. An angel is a finite being. He cannot perform miracles. The miracle at Bethsaida was not the angel's doing, but God's. A miracle is something done by God, and only God, outside the order of all created nature. God performs all miracles. He may use angels or saints as instruments to cause the miracles.

ANGELS OF THE LORD

Chapter Seven: Angel's Names

We don't know if every angel has a proper name. The Bible mentions only three who have proper names—Michael, Gabriel, and Raphael. All others are known by their activities and their position in the Nine Choirs of Angels. If they do have proper names they are undoubtedly too awesome and wonderful for our ears.

The angel who appeared before Samson's mother certainly did not reveal his name. She said in Judges 13:6: "A man of God came to me, having the countenance of an angel, very awful. And when I asked him who he was, and whence he came, and by what name he was called, he would not tell me."

Samson's father had the same experience. When an angel appeared to him he tried to find out the angel's name, saying: "What is thy name, that, if thy word shall come to pass, we may honor thee?"

The angel answered: "Why askest thou my name, which is wonderful?"

The patriarch Jacob didn't have any better luck. It was Jacob who wrestled with an angel. Jacob said, "Tell me by what name are thou called?"

The angel replied: "Why dost thou ask my name? And he blessed him in the same place."

There was a valid reason why angels did not offer their names to mortals. In those days idolatry was a real danger. Angels were careful not to let the people offer sacrifices to them. They did not want to be worshiped because only God was to be worshiped.

The problem of idolatry was far greater then than it is today. In fact, when Samson's father, Manue, saw the angel he started to make a sacrificial offering to him. That was one thing the angel did not want. He said to Manue, "If thou press me, I will not eat of thy bread, but if thou wilt offer a holocaust, offer it to the Lord."

Even Saint John the Evangelist had to be stopped from adoring an angel. John said: "And I, John, who have heard and seen these things. And, after I had heard and seen, I fell down to adore before the feet of the angel who showed me these things, and he said to me:

"See thou do it not, for I am thy fellow servant, and of thy brethren the prophets, and of them that keep the words of the prophecy of this book. Adore God, unto Thy altar above, before the face of Thy divine majesty."

This ties in with St. John's vision: "Another angel came, and stood before the altar, having a golden censer, and there was given to him much incense, that he should offer of the prayers of all saints upon the golden altar, which is before the throne of God. And the smoke of the incense of the prayers of the saints ascended up before God from the hand of the Angel."

We can ask for no better mediators than the angels.

"Ministers" or Masareth, and "Servants" or 'Ebhedh

The most important duty of angels is to minister to God and do His will. The Bible often refers to them as Servants of the Lord, and Ministers. You can find other synonyms such as "hosts" and "priests." According to St. Paul, the priest is "a minister of the holies, and of the true tabernacle, which the Lord hath pitched, and not man."

In Psalms 102:21 you find" "Bless the Lord, all ye his hosts: you ministers of His that do His will." And we find disturbing words about angels in Job 4:18 "Behold in His servants He puts no trust, and in His angels He finds folly."

"Watcher" or 'Ir

This is an appropriate word for angels because they never sleep and are forever on guard over us and are also ready to carry out God's commands. Being heavenly spirits, they have no need to rest.

However, the only place you will find the word "watcher" to describe an angel is in the book of Daniel: "I saw in the vision of my head upon my bed: and behold a watcher and a holy one came down from heaven." Elsewhere it says: "And whereas the king saw a watcher and a holy one come down from heaven, and say, Cut down the tree and destroy it, but leave the stump of the roots thereof in the earth."

"Host" or "Army" or Sabha

We are not to construe that the words "hosts" and "army" indicate anything warlike or that they mean there is military organization in heaven. The implication really is that the heavenly spirits are well organized and well ordered. In Psalms 148:2: "Praise ye Him all His angels; praise ye Him, all His hosts."

It is ironic that some of the greatest words in the Holy Scriptures were spoken by Satan. But what he said tells us how we may shield ourselves from his evil. Satan was talking to Job about God when he said: "Hast not thou made an hedge about Him, and about His house, and about all that He hath on every side? Thou hast blessed the work of His hands, and His substance in increased in the land" (Job 1:10).

Satan gives us the clue to our own salvation. We can pray to God for a hedge of angels to surround us and protect us from Satan. As for being saved, look to the Acts of the Apostles, when the Philipian jailer asked the Apostle Paul, "What must I do to be saved?"

Paul's answer was incredibly simple: "Believe on the Lord Jesus Christ, and thou shalt be saved" (Acts 16:30,31).

The statement is so simple that many of us may misread it. Yet, all that is being said is that you must believe in the Lord Jesus Christ as your own personal Saviour. You don't have to do anything else. You don't have to straighten out your life first. You don't have to give up any habits. You don't have to go through any ridiculous cleansing process first.

You come as you are. The leper came as he was. The blind man came as he was. The thief on the Cross came as he was.

Once you are saved, you can then pray for that glorious hedge to of angels to protect you from Satan's evils.

ANGELS OF THE LORD

Chapter Eight: Angels and Our Founding Fathers

Naturally, all loyal Americans believe that this is the greatest nation under the sun. Interestingly, the history of the United States is full of instances where our founding fathers apparently were divinely inspired when they needed help the most. In a number of cases, as we shall see, the early leaders of this country actually met and conversed with or were given prophetic visions through the courtesy of God's angels.

The Great Seal

How many of you have ever looked at the back of a dollar bill and wondered where the Great Seal of the United States came from? Virginia F. Brasington did some research into the matter and was startled at what she discovered. From what she found out there is every indication that an angel was directly involved in its inception. Let's quote from her book *Flying Saucers in the Bible*:

"Speaking of the Great Seal of the United States, there is a mystery connected with it. Let's look at it a moment. It has an eagle on the obverse (front) side, and an Egyptian pyramid on the other, or reverse, side. On the obverse side, the circle above the head of the eagle has thirteen "pieces argent"; the breast has a shield with thirteen stripes; the right talon holds an olive branch with thirteen arrows. The Latin words, "E Pluribus Unum," is on the ribbon around the neck, and is translated, "out of many one," or "One out of many," meaning, of course, one union out of many states. On the reverse side is an unfinished Egyptian pyramid. The capstone is above it, not yet put in place, and the "glory", or burst of light surrounding it, contains an eye, symbolic of the all-seeing eye of God; and the words, "Annuit Coptis", above it, which translated means, "He (God) has prospered our beginnings." The numerals at the base are "1776". Below this are the words, "Novis Ordo Seclorum", meaning, "A New Order of the Ages", or "A mighty order of the ages lives anew", or "An ancient order is born again."

"All of this is odd. How did an Egyptian pyramid get on our most significant symbol? This Great Seal is applied to about 3,000 documents annually, including presidential proclamations, ratifications of treaties, commissions of cabinet members and ambassadors, etc., on which documents only the obverse side of the Seal probably the most common piece of exchange we have."

Do you know who designed this Great Seal? Of course you don't. Neither does anyone else. The Continental Congress had asked Benjamin Franklin, Thomas Jefferson, and John Adams to arrange for a seal for the United States Of America (then consisting of only thirteen states). Well, the three men met and conferred, and pondered. None of the designs they created, or which were submitted to them were suitable. The time was drawing close when they must submit their final design.

Fairly late at night, after working on the project all day, Jefferson walked out into the cool night air of the garden to clear his mind. In a few minutes he rushed back into the room, crying jubilantly, "I have it! I have it!" Indeed, he did have some plans in his hands. They were the plans showing the Great Seal as we know it today.

Asked how he got the plans, Jefferson told a strange story. A man approached him wearing a black cloak that practically covered him, face and all, and told him that he (the strange visitor) knew they were trying to devise a seal, and that he had a design which was appropriate and meaningful. Jefferson liked the plans immediately, and was in such a hurry to show them to the other two that he rushed back into the house without even saying, "Thank you", to the stranger.

After the excitement died down, the three went out into the garden to find the stranger, but he was gone. Thus, neither these founding fathers, nor anybody else, ever knew just who really designed the great seal of the United States!

Washington's Vision

One of the greatest prophetic visions of all times was experienced by none other that our first president. George Washington foresaw the future of this land when an angel appeared in front of him as he prayed. The story was first published some years after Washington's death and originated with one Anthony Sherman who had served in Washington's personal forces at Valley Forge. The vision is exciting and highly accurate—and came directly from the Lord. We quote the words of Mr. Sherman in full as not to lose any of these thrilling, historical moments:

ANGELS OF THE LORD

"From the opening of the Revolution we experienced all phases of fortune, now good and now ill, one time victorious and another conquered. The darkest period we had, I think was when Washington, after several reverses, retreated to Valley Forge, where he resolved to pass the winter of 1777. Ah, I have often seen the tears coursing down our dear commander's careworn cheeks, as he would be conversing with confidential officers about the condition of his poor soldiers. You have doubtless heard the story of Washington's going to the thicket to pray. Well, it was not only true, but he used often to pray in secret for aid and comfort from God, the interposition of whose Divine Providence brought us safely through the darkest days of tribulation.

"One day, I remember it well, the chilly wind whistling through the leafless trees, though the sky was cloudless and the sun shone brightly, he remained in his quarters nearly all afternoon alone.

"When he came out I noticed that his face was a shade paler than usual, and there seemed to be something on his mind of more than ordinary importance. Returning just after dusk, he dispatched an orderly to the quarters of an officer, who was presently in attendance. After a preliminary conversation of about half an hour, Washington gazing upon his companion with that strange look of dignity which he alone could command, said:

"I do not know whether it is owing to the anxiety of my mind or what, but this afternoon, as I was sitting at this table engaged in preparing a dispatch, something seemed to disturb me. Looking up, I beheld standing opposite a singularly beautiful female. So astonished was I, for I had given strict orders not to be disturbed, that it was some moments before I found language to inquire the purpose of her presence. A second, a third, and even a fourth time did I repeat my question, but received no answer from my mysterious visitor, except a slight raising of her eyes. By this time I felt strange sensations spreading through me. I would have risen, but the riveted gaze of the being before me rendered volition impossible. I assayed once more to address her, but my tongue had become useless. Even thought itself had become paralyzed. A new influence, mysterious, potent, irresistible, took possession of me. All I could do was to gaze steadily, vacantly at my unknown visitant. Gradually the surrounding atmosphere seemed filled with sensations, and grew luminous. Everything about me seemed to rarify; the mysterious visitor becoming more airy and yet more distinct to my sight than before. I now began to feel as one dying, or rather to experience the sensation which I have sometimes imagined accompanies dissolution. I did not think, I did not reason. I did not move. All, alike, were impossible. I was only conscious of gazing fixedly, vacantly, at my companion.

"Presently, I heard a voice saying, 'Son of the Republic, look and learn.' When at the same time my visitor extended her arm eastwardly, I now beheld a heavy white vapor at some distance rising fold upon fold. This gradually dissipated, and I looked upon a strange scene. Before me lay spread out in one vast plain all the countries of the world, Europe, Asia, Africa and America. I saw rolling and tossing between Europe and America the billows of the Atlantic, and between Asia and America lay the Pacific. 'Son of the Republic,' said the same mysterious voice as before 'look and learn.' At that moment I beheld a dark shadowy being like an angel standing, or rather floating in mid-air between Europe and America. Dipping water out of the ocean in the hollow of each hand, he sprinkled some upon America with his right hand, while with his left hand he cast some on Europe. Immediately a dark cloud raised from these countries, and joined in mid-ocean. For awhile it remained stationary and then moved slowly westward, until it enveloped America in its murky folds. Sharp flashes of lightning gleamed through it at intervals, and I heard the smothered groans and cries of the American people. A second time the angel dipped water from the ocean, and sprinkled it as before. The dark cloud was then drawn back to the ocean, in whose heaving billows it sank from view. A third time I heard the mysterious voice saying, 'Son of the Republic, look and learn. 'I cast my eyes upon America and beheld villages and towns and cities springing up one after another until the whole land, from the Atlantic to the Pacific, was dotted with them. Again I heard the mysterious voice say, 'Son of the Republic, the end of the century cometh, (1800) Look and learn.'

"And with this, the dark, shadowy figure turned its face southward and from Africa I saw an ill-omened spectre approach our land. It flitted slowly over every town and city of the latter. The inhabitants presently set themselves in battle array against each other. As I continued looking, I saw a bright angel on whose brow rested a crown of light on which was traced the word 'Union,' place an American flag between the divided nation, and say, 'Remember, ye are brethren.' Instantly, the inhabitants, casting from them their weapons, became friends once more, and united around the national standard.

"Again I heard the mysterious voice saying, 'Son of the Republic, look and learn.' At this the dark, shadowy angel placed a trumpet to his mouth and blew three distinct blasts; and taking water from the ocean, he sprinkled it upon Europe, Asia and Africa. Then my eyes beheld a fearful scene: from each of these countries arose thick, black clouds that were soon joined into one. And throughout this mass there gleamed a dark-red light, by which I saw hordes of armed men, who, moving with the cloud, marched by land and sailed by sea to America; which country was enveloped in the volume of the cloud. And I dimly saw these vast armies devastate the whole country and burn the villages, towns and cities that I beheld springing up.

"As my ears listened to the thundering of the cannon, the clashing of swords, and the shouts and cries of millions in mortal combat, I again heard the mysterious voice saying, 'Son of the Republic, look and learn.' As the voice ceased, the shadowy angel, for the last time, dipped water from the ocean and sprinkled it upon America. Instantly the dark cloud rolled back, together with the armies it had brought, leaving the inhabitants of the land victorious.

"Then once more I beheld the villages, towns and cities springing up where I had seen them before; while the bright angel, planting the azure standard he had brought into the midst of them, cried in a loud voice: 'While the stars remain and the heavens send down dew upon the earth, so long shall the Union last.' And taking the crown on which was blazoned the word 'Union,' he placed it upon the standard, while people kneeling down said 'Amen.'

"The scene began to fade and dissolve and I at last saw nothing but the rising, curling vapor I at first beheld. This also disappearing, I found myself once more gazing upon the mysterious visitor who, in the same voice I had heard before said, 'Son of the Republic, what you have seen is thus interpreted. Three great perils will come upon the Republic. The most fearful for her is the third; but the whole world united shall not prevail against her. Let every child of the Republic learn to live for his God, his land, and his Union.' With those words the vision vanished, and I started from my seat and felt that I had seen a vision; wherein had been shown me the birth, progress and destiny of the United States."

"Such my friend," continued the venerable narrator, "were the words I heard from Washington's own lips; and America will do well to profit by them."

Chapter Nine: Lucifer, the Ex-Angel

He is now called Satan, or the devil, but at one time he was "Lucifer, the son of the morning." It is believed that at one time he was an archangel, with Michael. That was before he was cast out of heaven with his rebel forces. Unfortunately, Lucifer still fights. He still wins too often against the forces of good. There are times when it appears that he is also winning the war. But that can never, be. Eventually, God will win. Satan will be stripped of his dark powers forever.

The very existence of Lucifer indicates that God's universe is not perfect. How can something be considered perfect when this great conflict between good and evil exist? It's a mystery. In fact, the Apostle Paul calls it "the mystery of iniquity" in II Thessalonians 2:7.

In reality, we know very little about what transpired in heaven. Information is scarce. According to II Peter 2:4, we learn: "God spared not the angels that sinned but cast them down into hell, and delivered them into chains of darkness, to be reserved unto judgment."

Jude 6 tells us that "The angels kept not their first estate, but left their own habitation."

When Did It All Happen?

If you said it happened between the dawn of creation and when Satan visited Adam and Eve in the Garden of Eden, you would not be far off.

Dante, the poet, thought the fall came within twenty seconds of the angels' creation. The upheaval began, says Dante, when Lucifer refused to wait for the time when he would be permitted to have perfect knowledge. Other scholars, like Milton, for instance, feel that the great fall came just before the creation of the Garden of Eden.

In any event, we can be sure that there has never been a catastrophe in the universe to match Lucifer's defiance of God, the fall into disgrace, and the taking of perhaps one-third of all of the angels into wickedness with him.

ANGELS OF THE LORD

War In Heaven

"War" is the only word that can be used to describe the turmoil that took place in heaven when Satan (Lucifer) rebelled. It was said that Lucifer was the most beautiful of all angels. Undoubtedly, he was God's second in command, the ruling prince of the universe.

The war in heaven began when Lucifer sinned. Until that time Lucifer was considered an angel of light. Ezekiel tells us in 28:12-17: "You had the seal of perfection, full of wisdom and perfect in beauty. You were the anointed cherub who covers, and I place you there. You were on the holy mountain of God. You walked in the midst of the stones of fire. You were blameless in your ways from the day you were created, until unrighteousness was found in you...Your heart was lifted up because of your beauty; you corrupted your wisdom by reason of your splendor."

Lucifer's rebellion was the start of the war in heaven. It continues now on earth and the climax is expected to come at Armageddon, when Christ and his angels will be victorious.

How do we know that one-third of all the angels followed Lucifer into hell? A clue comes from John, who tells us that the Scripture sometimes refers to angels as stars (Lucifer was the star of the morning). In Revelation 12:4, John says: "His tail swept away a third of the stars of heaven and threw them to the earth."

Apostle Paul says that Lucifer is "the prince of the power of the air, the spirit now worketh in the children of disobedience."

We must also remember that the rite of baptism in the Catholic Church includes an exorcism designed to cast out a demon in the baby. The priest may say that no one can be sure that a demon is in the baby, but if one is there, the exorcism will get rid of it. This is a necessary precaution. Any Catholic can baptize a baby if the baby is in danger of losing its life, but that is not enough after the baby survives. It must also take part in the official baptism by a priest to be sure of being cleansed of a demon.

Lucifer's Ambition

Lucifer was not happy being second in command. He wanted to be the center of power. He forgot that the angels, himself included, were created to glorify God. He wanted all of the power and all of the glory. Lucifer wanted to be worshiped; he did not want to worship. Lucifer suffered two sins—the sin of pride and the sin of covetousness. His words are recorded in Isaiah 14: "I will exalt my throne above the stars of God. I will sit upon the mount of the congregation. I will ascend above the heights of the clouds. I will be like the most high."

Lucifer had a lust for what belonged to God alone.

Today, the war still rages. Satan and his demons who were once angels are forever working their evil against us. They work to undermine the individual, the family, the nations and the world. There is never a cease-fire in the battle. Satan is determined to destroy the human race which God so loves.

This is a premise our world leaders don't seem to understand, or care to understand. There can be no everlasting peace in the world until they recognize that a far greater catastrophe occurred in heaven, and that peace will finally come only when they realize that Satan must be cast from earth the same way he was cast from heaven.

You can recognize Satan in the wars he starts, the discord he promotes, the hatred he engenders, the murders he initiates, the sins he urges us to commit, his opposition to God and to His commandments.

His ambition is to destroy nations, to lower and corrupt moral standards and to waste as many human resources as he can.

His goal is to crush the kingdom of God.

Although it does appear at times that he is succeeding in all of his devious endeavors, he will not win the war against righteousness. God is the stronger of the two. His army of angels is at least two-thirds as large as Satan's.

Satan's Tools

The tool Lucifer has used since the world began is his effort to discredit the word of God. Whenever his effort is successful, we find mankind suffering from a lack of strength and the loss of comfort which faith gives us.

Satan uses every trick available to make God look like a liar. He did it in the Garden of Eden when, disguised as a serpent, he asked: "Hath God said, Ye shall not eat of every tree of the garden?"

The reply was: "You shall not eat of the fruit of the tree which is in the midst of the garden...lest you die."

And in Genesis 3:4 we are told that Satan tried to make God out as a liar by saying, "ye shall not surely die." What he was trying to do was to convince the first couple that God did not know what He was talking about, that He was just giving Adam and Eve a senseless test.

So he raised a doubt in the minds of Adam and Eve, a tool that he has been using ever since. And Eve began to consider that maybe the serpent was right. After all, the fruit was pleasant to look at.

What real harm could come of merely testing it? She tasted it and encouraged Adam to do the same.

Satan had won. The unfortunate thing is that he won the most important battle of all. Our world today would have been a paradise if Adam and Eve had not doubted the word of God. Instead, the couple saw themselves banished from the Garden. They saw their son Abel lie dead at their feet. They saw many trials and tribulations in their lives before death took them.

Satan's tools are also our own senses. He uses them like wide avenues to reach us. Take our appetites of the flesh, for example. He jumps with glee when he arouses our lusts! He is overjoyed when he sees us make gluttons of ourselves. He is delirious when he watches us abuse our bodies and minds with alcohol and drugs. And when we sin against others he is ecstatic.

The fight against Satan is constant. It won't be resolved until Armageddon.

Chapter Ten: Demonic Cults

We are suddenly fascinated in a morbid way with the devil and his demons. Check with any bookstore, any newsstand , and you will see entire rows of books and magazines devoted to the occult, Satan worship and demonic possession. Hollywood films and television scenarios abound on the subjects. Some polls tell us that 70 percent of Americans believe in a personal devil. In one poll conducted by Walter Cronkite over the CBS network, it was announced that the number of Americans who now believe in a personal devil has increased by 12 percent.

The irony in all of this is that 25 years ago it was predicted by scientists, psychologists, sociologists and some theologians that interest in such matters in the next generation would die out. How wrong they were!

It would appear that the devil is having his day, at least in the entertainment medium. Look at your local newspaper and see the number of films being advertised. You'll see such offerings as sadism, demon possession, devil worship and horror.

Unfortunately, we find similar writings among both Catholic and Protestant writers. It's as though the devil has become a fad, and everyone is pouncing on him to capture the attention of the public.

It is also unfortunate that the devil and his demons are real beings constantly at work in the real world around us. That there are now increases in Satanic activity may indicate that the Second Coming is near. The New Testament reveals how Satan and his emissaries worked incredibly hard to defeat Jesus Christ. And today it would appear that he is winning, or at least stepping up his activities to such an extent that peace seems to be eluding nearly every nation on earth.

Demonic Possession

Many psychiatrists are now of the firm opinion that when a patient can't be helped he may be possessed. These doctors are at last realizing that the devil does have power on earth and that to affect a cure for some of their patients, they must unite with priests and other experts who are adept at removing demons from the bodies of the mentally ill.

Dr. Kenneth McCall is an authority on Satanism. At one time he was a noted British surgeon in China until he was forced to return to England. He took up psychiatry but soon learned that there were hundreds of patients who could not be helped by psychiatry or even the surgeon's scalpel.

Dr. McCall recalled his days in China. There, he had witnessed demonism first hand and wondered now if these hundreds of patients who defied a cure were similarly afflicted.

At this time, the late Bishop of Exeter had joined a special task force to deal with the problem. Dr. McCall joined the group, too, and is now an international figure who acts as a liaison between the medical profession, the International Fraternity of Psychiatrists, and the church on problems that have to do with Satanism, demon possession and exorcism.

Many religious leaders feel that the occult is nothing to play around with. There are frequent accounts in the press about cases of demon inspired crimes including murder. Even those who have studied psychic phenomena would warn that one should be ready to protect himself against the forces of darkness. Even those mediums and sensitives who are not afraid of the devil are apt to take certain precautions before attempting to establish contact with the spirit kingdom. According to both clairvoyants and UFO contactees there is a war going on throughout the cosmos between "good" and "evil" and this battle has been going on for eons. Pope Paul stated some years ago that he was convinced that the devil was on the attack at every level of society.

Are UFOs Angels?

The idea is not original with the authors. Many Christian writers feel that unidentified flying objects may well be a part of God's visible angels who are devoted to watch over the physical affairs of His universe. It is, of course, a matter of conjecture.

The possibility is strong, however, when you consider that on a purely practical basis, UFOs could not come from another planet. The nearest planet which could sustain life is four and a half light years away from earth. A space ship would have to travel four and a half years at the speed of light to reach us. For that reason, many people are turning now to the supernatural as a possible reason for the existence of UFOs.

These unexplained sightings have been with us ever since recorded history. The fact that they are now occurring with greater frequency than ever may mean something.

A typical example of the mystery behind UFOs occurred in Japan on January 15, 1975. A squadron of objects soared across the skies over half the length of Japan. There were between 15 and 20 of these UFO-like objects flying inside a strange mist.

Telephone switchboards at police stations and government installations were jammed with calls. Thousands of people saw the objects, including government and police officials. The squadron was sighted and reported in cities several hundreds of miles apart in less than an hour.

Duty officer Takeo Ohira said, "All the callers reported seeing a huge cloud passing over the city. They said they saw strange objects inside the cloud moving in a straight line."

Professor Hiroshi Mayazawa said they were not planes "because no planes or natural phenomena appeared on my radar. It was an exceptionally clear night. To me the whole thing is a mystery."

The professor saw the objects from the Control Room of Tokyo's Meteorological Bureau station near the airport. He said, "I was mystified. Nothing showed up on my radar. I reported my sighting to the airport control tower and they told me that nothing showed up on their radar either."

UFOs or angels? Similar sightings are reported on every continent. According to the experts, for every one in twenty sightings there is no satisfactory scientific explanation. Theories and the imaginative explanations of some experts are found wanting.

The fact that the UFOs did not show up on radar screens is significant. Since angels are not of flesh and blood, but are spiritual, it becomes understandable why blips did not appear. There was simply nothing solid or tangible for the radar waves to hit and bounce back from.

We don't imply that every sighting represents an angel or angels going about their universal chores. In fact, some unidentified flying objects have been picked up on radar screens. The sightings over the capitol dome in Washington in the 1950's is a good example. However, we don't know of any other explanation for them that comes as close to the truth as the angel theory.

You can find passages in Isaiah, Ezekiel, Zechariah and the Book of Revelation in which to draw all the parallels you wish.

Look to Ezekiel 10: "Each of the four cherubim had a wheel beside him—'The Whirl-Wheels,' as I heard them called, for each one had a second wheel crosswise within, sparkled like chrysolite, giving off a greenish-yellow glow. Because of the construction of these wheels, the cherubim could go straight forward in each of four directions; they did not turn when they changed directions but could go in any of the four ways their faces looked....and when they rose into the air the wheels rose with them, and stayed beside them as they flew. When the cherubim stood still, so did the wheels, for the spirit of cherubim was in the wheels."

The last part of Ezekiel's statement is fascinating: the spirit of the cherubim was in the wheels." Is it too far-fetched to assume that the spirits of the angels are in the heavenly machines they fly?

An Astronomer's Vision

Though scientists may not want to admit that such things as angel's exist, they too have been touched by these messengers of the Lord. One astronomer tells of the marvelous sight of viewing gigantic angels deep in space as seen through a telescope.

His journal written in the late eighteen hundreds reveals this amazing testimony. The astronomer expresses his feeling that the vision was of the angel of death, since his observation was made just prior to a plague that swept Europe. Here is his account:

"It was during the prevalence of the great cholera plague to which I refer that I was invited by a few gentlemen, who were in sympathy with my mystical studies, to join them in a select party, the aim of which was to make astronomical experiments under peculiarly favorable circumstances. I do not feel at liberty to mention the names of those who graced our little gathering; it is enough to state that they were all distinguished for their scientific attainments. At a certain period of the night we adjourned to an observatory, where we were to enjoy the rare privilege of making observations through an immense telescope, constructed under the direction of Lord Rosse. When my turn arrived for viewing the heavens through this wonderful piece of mechanism, I confess I beheld a sight which for a long time held me breathless. At first I saw only the glorious face of the spangled firmament, with that sense of mingled awe and reverence which never forsakes the mind of the most accustomed observer when he exchanges the view of the black vault of midnight, with its thinly scattered field of distant lamps checkering the heavens, for the gorgeous mass of divine pyrotechnics which bursts upon the sight through the dazzling revealments of the magic telescope. Breathless, transfigured, whirled away from a cold, dim, cloudy world to a land— not of fairies or angels, but of gods and demigods— to skies burning and blazing with millions of suns, double suns, star roads, and empyrean walls, in which the bricks and mortar are sparkling suns and glowing systems, miracle of miracles! I hold my breath and tremble as I think, for the sight never grows old nor familiar to me, and every time I have thus gazed, it has only been to find the awe and wonder deepen.

"Absorbed as I was in contemplating the immensity and brilliancy of this ever new and ever gorgeous spectacle, in about forty seconds, I found a singular blur coming between the shining frame of the heavens and the object glass. I was about to draw back, deeming some accidental speck had fallen upon the plane of vision, when I was attracted by observing that what I had deemed to be a blur actually assumed the shape of a human profile, and was, even as I gazed, in the act of moving along in space between the glass and the heavens. Fascinated and wonder struck, I still retained the calm and fixed purpose of continuing my observations, and in this way I say, yes! I distinctly saw a gigantic and beautifully proportioned human face sail by the object-glass, intercepting the view of the stars and maintaining a position in mid-air which I should judge to have been some five miles above the earth's surface.

"Allowing for the immense magnifying powers of the instrument, I could not conceive of any being short of a giant whose form would have covered whole acres of space, to whom this enormous head could have appertained. When I first beheld this tremendous apparition, it seemed to be sailing perpendicularly in the air, intercepting, the field of vision just between myself and the planet to which the glass was pointed. I have subsequently seen it four times, and on each occasion, though the face was the same, the inclination of the form must have varied, sometimes floating horizontally, at another time looking down as if from a height, and only permitting a partial view of the features, greatly foreshortened, to appear. Still again I have seen it as at first and finally, it sailed by in such a fashion in the wake of the beautiful head, the whole apparition occupying at least a hundred seconds in passing the glass, during which period the sight of all other objects but this sailing, dense mass was entirely obscured. On the occasion I at first alluded to, I became so fixed with astonishment and doubt, that I should not have mentioned what I saw had not the figure returned and from the side where it had disappeared I beheld it slowly, gradually, unmistakably float by the object-glass with even more distinctness than at first. This second time I could perceive as unequivocally as if I had been gazing at my own reflection in a mirror, the straight, aquiline cast of features, the compressed lip, and stern expression of the face, the large glittering eye, fixed like a star upon the earth beneath, and long lashes like a fringe of beams, falling upon the side of the face. When I had fully unquestionably satisfied myself that what I had seen was a reality, I withdrew from the instrument, then requested one of the company present to examine my pulse and report upon its action. 'Moderate and firm,' was the reply, given in a tone of curious inquiry; 'but you look somewhat pale, Chevalier. May we not know what has occurred to disturb you?' Without answering, I proceeded carefully to examine the glass, and to scrutinize all its parts and surroundings with a view of endeavoring to find some outside cause for what I must else have deemed a hallucination.

"I was perfectly familiar with the use, capacity and arrangement of the telescope and as neither within nor without the instrument, nor yet in the aspect of the cloudless sky could I find the least possible solution to my difficulty. I determined to resolve the occurrence into the convenient word I have just used and set the matter down as hallucination. But my friends were not so easily satisfied. At last, one of them, an old and very venerable scientist, whose opinions I had long been accustomed to regard with respect, looking steadily in my face, asked in a deep and earnest tone: 'Will you not tell us if you have seen anything unusual? We beg you to do so, Monsieur, and have our own reasons for the query.' Thus adjured, but still with some hesitation, I answered that I had certainly thought I had seen the outlines of a human face, and that twice, crossing the object-glass of the telescope.

"Never shall I forget the piercing look of intelligence interchanged by my companions at this remark. Without a word of comment, however, the one whose guest I had the honor to be, stepped to a cabinet in the observatory where he kept his memoranda, and drawing forth a package, he thus addressed me: 'What you may have seen tonight, Chevalier, I am not yet informed of, but as something remarkable appears to have struck you in the observation you have just made, we are willing to place ourselves at your mercy, and provided you will reciprocate the confidence we repose in you, we will herewith submit to you some memoranda which will convince you some of us at least, have beheld other bodies in space than suns and planets.' Before my honored entertainer could proceed further, I narrated to him as exactly as I could, the nature of what I had seen, and then confessed I was too doubtful of my own powers of observation to set down such a phenomenon as an actuality unless I could obtain corroborative evidence of its truth. 'Receive it, then, my friend,' cried my host, 'Good God! Then it must be true.'

"I dare not recall verbatim the wording of the notes I then heard read, as they were so mixed up with details of astronomical data, that the recital might serve to do that which I then solemnly promised to avoid namely, whilst publishing the circumstances I then heard of, for the benefit of those who might put faith in them, carefully to suppress the names of the parties who furnished me with the information. My friends then assured me that during the past six months, whilst conducting their observations at that place, they had, all on several occasions, seen human faces of gigantic proportions floating by the object-glass of their telescopes in almost the same fashion and with the same peculiarities of form and expression as the one I had just described. One gentleman added that he had seen three of these faces on one night, passing one after the other. For many successive weeks this party had stationed themselves at distant places, at given periods of time to see if the same phenomenon would appear to more than one observer at a time.

"Tuesday, June 4, 18-. Third night of watching. Took my station at the glass at 11:30 p.m. At 2 or just as the last vibration of the clock resounded from the observatory, the first outline of the head came into view. This time the form must have been directly perpendicular, for the sharp outline of the straight profile came into a direct line with the glass and enabled me to see a part of the neck and clear the top of the head. The figure was sailing due north and moved across the glass in 72 seconds, etc., etc.

"Memoranda 2. I began to despair of success as three days had now elapsed without any interruption of the kind anticipated in my observations. At ten minutes and three seconds to two, I began to experience an overpowering sense of fatigue and determined to close my observations at the moment my chronometer should strike the hour 2:30. The giant has just appeared; his head came into, view exactly as the clock was striking two, and placing my chronometer directly before me so as to catch the first glimpse of the time when he disappeared. I find that his transit occupied exactly seventy-two seconds.

"Tuesday, June 4, 18-. Titanus came into view at 2 o'clock precisely, sailed by in 1\Yi seconds, upright and face in profile, moving due north." etc., etc. Some of the observations recorded by the spectators of this phenomenon were full of emotion, my companions were so deeply moved and manifested such intense feeling on the subject of what they had seen, that the reading was several times interrupted, and one of the party remarked, he believed he should be disposed to shoot anyone who should presume to cast doubt or ridicule on a subject which had affected them all so deeply.

"For the next fortnight I enjoyed the privilege of spending a considerable portion of each night in that observatory. Twice the strange phantom sailed before my view in one week. By permission of my friends, I changed my station and continued my anxious watch with another instrument. On the second night I beheld the Titanic head with even more distinctness than before, and three of my fellow watchers shared the weird spectacle with me from different posts of observation. One week later, I determined to avail myself of a final observation with one of the most superb instruments ever constructed. For many hours my exhaustive watch was unsuccessful; but then, two faces of the same size and expression, the one slightly in advance of, and measurably shading the other, sailed slowly, very slowly into view. They passed on with an unappreciable, gentle motion. The companion who shared my watch had pointed his glass a little more to the east than mine, and I had but time to murmur an injunction for him to change it as the figures came into view. He saw them, however, just as they were passing out of the field of vision and exclaimed, "By heavens! there are two of them!"

"Some years after this memorable night I received a letter from one of my associates in this weird secret, according to me the permission I sought, namely, to publish the circumstances I have related thus far, but carefully to withhold the witnesses' names. In answer to my query whether my correspondent had again seen the tremendous phantom of the skies, he replied in the negative, adding: "Call me superstitious or what you will; the whole history lays us open to ourselves and to each other, to such wild suggestions and inconceivable possibilities, that no hypothesis can seem so improbable as that we should all be correct. I will venture to hint to you, one of us, you know, that I have somehow always connected the apparitions in question with the prevalence of the cholera. It was immediately in advance of this pestilence, and during the time when it raged, that we all saw them. Since that period we have never again beheld them, that is, none of us who now remain on earth.

"These appearances ceased with the pestilence and came with it. Could they have been the veritable destroying angels, think you? You, who are a mystic, should be able to answer me. I, with all my materialism, am so terribly shaken when I recall the terrific reality that I endeavor to banish its remembrance whenever it recurs to me."

Chapter Eleven: Are Angels to be Worshiped?

To do so would be a breach of the first commandment. We are warned not to worship the creature, only the creator. Unfortunately, too many people have a tendency to venerate angels. They look upon the angelic beings as gods, which is not as it should be. People pray to angels rather than pray with them. Only God should be the object of our worship and prayer.

Angels are mightier than men, and have the power to make themselves visible if God so wills it. Their purpose is to help work out our destinies as well as those of nations. They are closely linked with everything that happens on earth, and their knowledge of earthly matters far exceeds ours. Angels think, feel and display emotions. In Luke 15:10 of the Living Bible we learn that Jesus taught that "there is joy in the presence of angels of God when one sinner repents."

Angels Are Visible

General William Booth, founder of the Salvation Army, had a vision of angels. He said the rainbow of light around each angel was so brilliant that it had to be withheld, else he would not have been able to look at them.

The angel who rolled away the stone from the tomb of Jesus was dressed in white and his dazzling brilliance was like the flashing lightning....No man could look at it. And even the guards at the tomb were struck dumb. They were stiffened as though dead. And the stone that weighed a lot more than any one man could handle was easily rolled aside by the spiritual being.

Biblical personages had no trouble recognizing angels. Lot, Jacob, Abraham and Daniel knew them on sight. Daniel and John describe them as being exquisitely brilliant, like the sun, with beauty that is impossible to describe.

Then there were the three Hebrew children, Shadrach, Meshach, and Abednego who refused to worship the king of Babylon. When they did not bow, they were thrown into the fire to be burned alive. But that did not happen because an angel protected them from the flames, so much so that not even their garments were singed. But the king looked into the flames and said, "I see four men...in the midst of the fire" (Daniel 3:25).

We See Angels, But Don't Know It

Yes, angels are visible quite often, only they don't appear to us as spiritual beings, but rather as men, and even as strangers.

You've read the newspaper accounts frequently. A man, a woman or a child is in mortal danger and is rescued by a man who disappeared into the crowd of onlookers after the rescue is complete. He's gone. No one can find him. Many say they saw him and describe him as being an ordinary looking person. But he seems to have vanished. Reporters want a statement. The rescued person wants to thank him. Is it too far-fetched to assume that the ordinary looking person was an angel? Of course not.

Angels are visible, but fortunately for us they come in the guise of men. They come when they are needed. The man, or woman, you pass on the street may be an angel bent on doing some good for someone that can't be accomplished in his invisible state.

God Withholds His Angels

More often than not, God keeps his angels from interfering with the evil in the world. He did so even in the early days of Christianity when Christians were thrown to the lions. He did so again when His only Son was on the Cross. There were no angelic armies of deliverance to aid Jesus. The angels merely stood poised for action, unable to interfere because God did not want them to.

You can check world history to see the great famines, disasters, catastrophes, the terrible blights that visited man. Angels stood ready, but were not given the word. Why? Why doesn't God send His angels to punish the sinners, to alleviate the suffering? The answer is that God will do so when the time is right. We will know it as the Second Coming. When the great conflict between good and evil comes to a climax, then the angelic armies will descend with all the fury of a thousand nuclear explosions.

ANGELS OF THE LORD

Angels in the Grandstand

The angels are watching us! If you stray from living the Christian life, think about who is watching what you are doing. You have a host of angels keeping tabs on you, and that thought should motivate you toward Christian ways. For instance, Paul charged Timothy that angels were constantly watching to see how he served Jesus and lived cleanly. In the Amplified Bible, 1 Timothy 5:21: (Paul says) "I solemnly charge you in the presence of God and of Jesus Christ and of the chosen angels, that you guard and keep (these rules)."

In Hebrews 12:1 the angels are described as "a great cloud of witnesses." In addition, Dr. Vance Havner in his book, ***Though I Walk Through the Valley***," tells of a preacher who worked far into the night on a sermon that would be preached only to a very small congregation.

His wife, probably annoyed, wondered why he spent so much time on it since so few would hear it. The preacher replied, "You forget, my dear, how large my audience will be."

Dr. Havner stated: "Nothing is trivial here if heaven looks on. We shall play a better game if 'seeing we are encompassed,' we remember who is in the grandstand!"

The Reaper Is Not Grim

We in our natural world are separated from the spiritual world by a thin veil. The veil is death. Paul calls it "the last enemy." Perhaps calling it "the last battle" would be more apt. It is a battle, a profound crisis event. But once the cord is broken we become free of our mortal prison and rise up, with the help of ministering angels, to a greater kingdom.

Just as Jesus was escorted into heaven by angels, so will we find our trip guided by angels, or at least one angel and probably the one who stood guard over us for so many decades. Evangelist D.L. Moody was privileged to see heaven before he died. He was on his death bed and knew death was near. He said, "Earth recedes, heaven opens before me."

At first, witnesses thought that he was dreaming, or that he was hallucinating. However, it was neither of those. Moody himself said, "No this is no dream...it is beautiful, it is like a trance. If this is death, it is sweet. There is no valley here. God is calling me and I must go."

The evangelist was given up for dead at that moment, but the prognosis was wrong. Moody revived and became strong enough to relate what he had seen on the other side. He told listeners that he had been "within the gates and beyond the portals." He had seen faces that were familiar, faces he had "loved long since and lost awhile."

Then the evangelist said: "Some day you will read in the papers that D.L. Moody of East Northfield is dead. Don't you believe a word of it. At that moment I shall be more alive than I am now. I shall have gone up higher that is all—out of this old clay tenement into a house that is immortal, a body that death cannot touch, that sin cannot taint, a body fashioned like unto His glorious body.... That which is born of the flesh may die. That which is born of the spirit will live forever." These words were written in the book, "*The Life of Dwight L. Moody*," by W.R. Moody.

Moody did not mention the presence of angels at his death, apparently, because they were not needed during his glimpse into the next world. However, the maternal grandmother of famed evangelist Billy Graham does. According to Rev. Graham, the room in which the woman lay dying suddenly filled with a heavenly light. It lasted only an instance, but when it was gone, the woman sat up on her death bed and cried, "I see Jesus. He has His arms outstretched toward me. I see Ben (her husband who had died some years before), and I see the angels." Then she died.

A divinity student who lay on her death bed, and in the presence of a relative and two faculty members, was heard to say: "I see Jesus. I can hear the singing of the angels."

Unfortunately, today's terminal patients are so filled with drugs and pain-killers that their observations into the spiritual world are not articulated the way they once were. But what theologians agree to now is that death for those who believe in Christ can be a glorious experience. They feel, too, that the angels who escorted the dead into heaven are accompanied by other angels who stay behind to give solace and hope to the grieving relatives and friends. When David said: "Yea, though I walk through the valley of the shadows of death, I will fear no evil," (Psalms 23:4), he knew that no evil could touch him once he passed over into heaven.

There is no reason to dread the thought of death. Once the suffering has ended, you will be transmitted to a world without pain, evil, sin, hate, greed, and all of the other ugliness you had to deal with on earth.

So the reaper is not grim. Death is not a tragedy. Christians should look upon death the way the angels do, which is with joy. The angels know that death releases us from time and places us into eternity. They revel in our resurrection the same way they reveled in the resurrection of Jesus.

Time and again we are shown proof that a better world awaits us. The Reverend A.A. Talbot witnessed such an amazing event many years ago when he was a missionary in China. He sat at the bedside of a dying man, a Chinese Christian. Rev. Talbot was still grieving from the loss of his little daughter, Margaret Gay. He now faced another loss in his friend beside him.

Suddenly, the room was filled with the sweetest music the reverend had ever heard. He had no idea where it was coming from. He saw the dying man looking up and smiling radiantly. The man said: "I see Jesus standing at the right hand of God, and Margaret Gay is with Him."

Rev. Talbot then knew where the music came from...and where his dead friend had gone.

Angels Can't Preach The Gospel

At first glance it does seem strange that angels are not permitted to preach the gospel, but on closer examination you can begin to understand why. For one thing, angels are pure. They have never been seduced by sin. They don't know what it means to be separated from God because of sin. Therefore, how could they possibly do a creditable job of bringing the salvation experience to man?

God commanded the church to preach. Man must save man, not an angel. When God was asked what plan He had in mind if man failed to preach the gospel, God said: "I have no other plan."

Angels may assist preachers. They can do it through miraculous and corroborating signs. Missionaries in the last century and in the 18th Century have reported angelic assistance in getting the Lord's message across on many occasions. No angel can be the pastor of a church, although he can watch over a church. No angel can counsel, but he can help the counselor through prayer. Incredible as it sounds, men do have certain privileges that are denied the angels.

An Angel and Joseph's Dilemma

We know that Gabriel came to Mary to announce that she would give birth to Jesus the Christ. Gabriel could not preach the gospel to Mary because that task belonged to Jesus when He grew into manhood. But he could bear witness to what would be said by the Saviour and His followers through the ages. In a song Mary sang to Elizabeth she made it quite plain that she understood what Gabriel had told her. She knew that God Almighty was in her womb, that He had humbled Himself to dwell among men of the flesh, and that one day He would suffer for mankind.

But what about Joseph? Here was a down-to-earth, hard working young man who was engaged to be married. And now, suddenly, the girl he loved was pregnant. By whom he didn't know. He knew only that he was not the father because he and Mary had not consummated their relationship with sex.

Under Jewish law, Mary was obviously guilty of adultery because in those days engagements were legal. But was she guilty? That was Joseph's dilemma. Mary told him that the Holy Spirit had come upon her. She insisted that she had never had sexual relations with a man.

It was the custom of the day that such a woman would be put away, and Joseph thought seriously of doing it. But it was then that an angel came to Mary's rescue by appearing to Joseph in a dream.

You'll find in Matthew 1:20 that the angel told Joseph that everything Mary said was true, that the baby she carried was an incarnation and that it was to be named Jesus, who was the Son of God.

Remember, the angel was not permitted to preach to Joseph. But he did say to Joseph, "He shall save the people from their sins."

Now that is Holy Gospel, or good news, pure and simple. Yet, technically, the angel was merely bearing witness to the gospel. The gospel was not preached until Jesus preached it, so that the angel only bore witness to what Jesus would say when He became a preacher.

Gabriel Prophesies

Gabriel came close to preaching when he appeared before David who was deep in prayer. Gabriel told him that sin is real and has to be paid for. He said the Messiah would do this by cutting off, or by being cut off, which meant that He would die for the sins of men. When that happens, Gabriel told David, the sin will no longer have the power to separate men from God.

You can see how close Gabriel came to preaching, but what he actually did was to make a prophesy.

The Angel and the Shepherds

In Mary's song, the Magnificat, we hear: "He hath put down the mighty from their seats, and exalted them of low degree. He hath filled the hungry with good things, and the rich He hath sent empty away. (Luke 1:52, 53).

What these words tell us is that God brought the message of Jesus' birth not to the rich and influential, but to the lowly. In fact, He brought it to the lowest of all occupations, the sheep- herder. These people were not educated. They had no money, no influence, no position. Yet, an angel appeared before them to announce the important event.

It takes no stretch of the imagination to understand what the sheepmen felt when they saw the angel. They were frightened, of course. Actually scared out of their wits.

But they were told again and again not to be afraid, that the angel came in peace. Nevertheless, the sight must have been awe-inspiring to say the least. Here were simple folks suddenly visited by a supernatural force that was far beyond their comprehension.

Eventually, the angel won them over. He was able to reassure them that he was not here to sit in judgment on them. He said he had a message for them. "For behold I bring you good tidings of great joy, which shall be to all people. For unto you born this day in the city of David, a Saviour, which is Christ the Lord." (Luke 2:10,11).

Here again we see that the angel did not preach a gospel, he merely announced an event. He had good news. The shepherds didn't need bad news. There was plenty of that everywhere. The angel said the good tidings, or good news was for everyone, for all people. The Saviour had come. He was truly needed. The people had lost their fellowship with God and the Saviour was here to bring them back into the fold.

The angel's message was clear. Sacrifices of goats and bulls did nothing. Their blood was spilled foolishly. But the blood of the Saviour? Now that was a different story.

Redemption was now possible. The Lord had come to earth to visit His people with salvation. And the angel brought his point home when he was suddenly accompanied by a multitude of heavenly hosts who began to sing, "Glory to God in the highest, and on earth peace, good will toward men."

What man in his right mind could still entertain doubts after such a heavenly display?

Angels—God's Middlemen

As we said earlier, angels know much more about man than we do. You might say it's their job to be ever alert to man's needs. And with their easy mobility they can be much more alert than we can. This is especially true when it comes to making sure that men are saved through the gospel.

Not all men know about the gospel. They are not disbelievers, but simply unbelievers. They are not aware that such incredible good news exists. Therefore, it is the task of the angels to make sure these people hear the gospel, so that Cornelius could be saved.

But Peter represented a problem. Cornelius was a Gentile, and as far as Peter was concerned, it was very wrong to preach the gospel for the salvation of Gentiles. Fortunately, the angel did not agree. He went to Cornelius and told him to send for Peter.

When that was done, God appeared to Peter in a dream and said it was perfectly all right to preach the gospel to a Gentile, or to anyone, for that matter. That was enough for Peter. He went to the Roman soldier, Cornelius, told the wonderful story of the gospel, and Cornelius was saved.

Considering all of the trouble involved, it would have been a lot simpler if the angel had taken Cornelius aside and preached the gospel. But that was not permitted. As we stated earlier, no angel knows first-hand the trials and tribulations of man because he has never experienced them. How can he then preach salvation when he himself has never had to concern himself with it?

Then there is the story of the Ethiopian nobleman who read the Bible but found himself completely baffled in the Old Testament. The section that confused him had to do with the Prophet Isaiah.

One would think that such a man, a nobleman of great authority, would be able to decipher the words, but he couldn't. Nor could anyone else tell him. Ah, but there was an angel nearby who heard the Ethiopian's plight. He could straighten the man out, if he were allowed to do so. But preaching the gospel was not allowed, not for any angel.

So the angel went to Philip and told him to go "toward the south unto the way that goeth down from Jerusalem unto Gaza, which is the desert." (Acts 8:26). Naturally, Philip obeyed.

Eventually, Philip came to a chariot holding the Ethiopian. He then interpreted the puzzling section of the Scripture to the

Ethiopian and also preached the gospel. Later, Philip baptized his new friend, who rode off rejoicing that he had been saved.

The story not only shows that angels are not allowed to preach, but that they are fully aware of our dilemmas, no matter what our faith, or even if we have no faith at all.

Angels and Jesus' Darkest Hours

There is no doubt at all that Jesus' most difficult period was His Crucifixion. However, a period which comes close to it was His temptation by Satan in the wilderness. Christ fasted for forty days and nights. Physically, he was in no condition to deal with the devil. And that was when Satan struck. He saw his chance to destroy the human race forever. The way Satan saw it, victory here would be greater even than the one he enjoyed in the Garden of Eden. The opportunity was exactly right. Jesus would be too weak to fight back. So the devil went on the attack.

His first thrust failed because Jesus quoted the Holy Scriptures. Satan's second attempt was thwarted because again Jesus quoted the Scriptures. After the third attack was lost to Satan for the same reason, "he (Satan) departed from Him (Jesus) for a season." (Luke 4:13).

At this point the angels came to Christ to assist Him. They did not help Him to resist Satan, as they help us. Jesus managed to do that on His own. As Matthew says 4:11, "Behold, angels came and ministered unto Him " They came to support Him in that trying period. Jesus Christ then knew and could sympathize with Christian believers for all ages to come, and lead them to victory over Satan in their hour of temptation.

The angels rarely left Jesus during His hour of torment before He was hung on the Cross. The night before He died He was in the Garden of Gethsemane. This was only a short time before His betrayal by Judas Iscariot.

His agony in the garden was so great that blood appeared where there should have been sweat. He had to call on an inner strength that no man had ever known. He knew that ahead of Him was a torment that no man had ever experienced. Jesus knew that He would have to place all the sins of man on His own shoulders.

For solace and encouragement, Jesus brought with Him into the Garden Peter, James and John. But they were of little help. They fell asleep, leaving Jesus alone. Jesus prayed, "Father, if thou be willing, remove this cup from me: nevertheless not my will, but thine, be done." (Luke 22:42).

It was then that an angel came to help, to strengthen Him. The Lord would have appreciated His disciples sharing His agony, instead He found the strength He needed in the presence of an angel.

Angels At The Cross

Twelve legions of angels with drawn swords were ready at an instant to come to Christ's aid if He so willed it. But that would have defeated His purpose. He stayed on the Cross, suffering excruciating pain because He knew that only through His death could the human race be saved. The hosts of angels were under strict orders to hover only and not interfere with Christ's purpose.

And again Satan struck in the representation of Christ's tormentors who cried, "If thou be the Son of God, come down from the cross." (Matthew 27:40).

Christ was fully aware of the fact that He could come down from the cross if He wanted to. He could also call on the angels to free Him from this living horror. But He would not let them come, not even to minister to Him. He stayed where He was, naked, nailed, bleeding, enduring the awful taunts of men below—and all for us.

We don't think much of sin today, but if we could have witnessed the agony of Christ we would come to understand the reason why the Lord refers to sin as the second largest thing in the world, the first being the love of God.

But think of what it must have been like for the angels who witnessed the Crucifixion! It was said that their consternation was such that they had to veil their faces. It was inconceivable to them that Jesus had to shoulder the fearful depravity of sin.

Then a great light appeared, shattering the darkness. The veils covering the angels' faces fell away. The light was salvation. The darkness was Satan, and he and his legions were again

defeated. Men would no longer be kept in darkness and defeat. Role of Angels at the Resurrection

ANGELS OF THE LORD

How heavy was the great boulder that sealed off Jesus' tomb? Bible students have pondered that question for ages, and they are not likely to ever find out. No matter, if Jesus wanted to come out on His own, without the assistance of angels, He could have. However, He knew the importance of drama, and what is more important or dramatic than seeing angels in all their blinding brilliance? The guards at the tomb saw them and were immediately paralyzed at the sight. They were well armed, but totally unable to lift their arms to fight.

And what did the guards see? Matthew 28:2-4 tells us: "And behold, there was a great earthquake for the angel of the Lord descended from heaven, and came and rolled back the stone from the door, and sat upon it. His countenance was like lightning, and his raiment white as snow: And for fear of Him the keepers did shake, and became as dead men."

It certainly must have been an awesome sight for the keepers to see a spiritual entity roll away the huge stone with just a touch of fingers.

And it was Mary who looked into the tomb and saw two more angels, one sitting at the head and the other at the feet of where Jesus lay. Then an angel outside the tomb said loud and clear: "He is not here, but is risen." (Luke 24:6).

Probably no mightier sentence has ever been uttered. It would eventually change the history of the world. Men could at last hope for a similar resurrection and a life everlasting in heaven.

Angels and the Ascension

"And when he had spoken these things, while they beheld, He was taken up; and a cloud received Him out of their sight." (Acts 1:9).

The disciples who watched this magnificent scene were beside themselves with grief. Their eyes were filled with tears.

But Jesus had not really forsaken them. He sent two angels who appeared like men. They were dressed in white. They went to the grieving disciples and said: "Ye men of Galilee, why stand ye gazing up into the heaven? This same Jesus, which is taken up from you into heaven." (Acts 1:11).

These angels remained behind to assure the disciples that they would always be near and always ready to help the Lord's people for ages to come.

Chapter Twelve: The Ministry of Angels in the Aquarian Age

"Angel Light" by Olivia Oribello

Angel in the sky,
Help me break away,
To be free of the lie.
Help me face another day,
Angel in the light,
So I can stand to stay

I'm fighting with all my might,
My struggles I pray you see,
To keep this glorious light.

Angel so near, smile upon me
And lend me an ear.
With your help I may see the sun,
And the light may be shared with everyone.
When your Light comes here
The battle will be won.

Angel in the Light,
Give me wisdom for the fight.
Keep me safe, till once again,
I join for the flight.

Angel in the Light,
Smile on me tonight.

ANGELS OF THE LORD

About William Alexander Oribello

Since 1965, Mr. Oribello has taught thousands of people how to improve their life in every way, through the proper application of the Mystical Sciences.

During childhood, he had many angelic visits. His many experiences have guided him to

first-hand encounters with both Inner Plane and Outer Living Adepts of the Secret Wisdom.

Mr. Oribello was an ordained minister with The Church of Divine Metaphysics. He made thousands of personal appearances giving lectures, workshops, praying and counseling with seekers of Truth from around the world. Through his writings and self-help cassettes, he has helped even more students and clients from all walks of life.

About Olivia Oribello

From a very early age, Olivia demonstrated a sincere interest and genuine gift in metaphysical subjects. She has trained very intensely with her father, William, since that time.

She gave her first lecture at a Spiritualist Church in Philadelphia at the age of six. She began writing articles and produced a meditation tape a year later. At the age of eight, she published her first poetry booklet.

Olivia has assisted in numerous workshops with her father from coast to coast, and has been used as a channel for spiritual healing and counseling to many people.

Olivia Oribello is a published poet (*the Arcadia Anthology of Poetry*) and is preparing herself for a career in Holistic Medicine, with emphasis on the integration of Body, Mind and Spirit.

■　　　■　　　■

By William Alexander Oribello

I believe in Angels. The word angel means "messenger." However, the Secret Teachings of all ages have revealed that angels or messengers exist in all dimensions of time and space. Let us explore these Dimensions of Angelic Existence.

At the top of the line, so to speak, are the angels of the highest spiritual world—what has been known as "Heaven" or the "Cosmic Planes": There are the Archangels who work with the will of Divine Providence. Under their direction are legions of beings, known simply as angels. The Biblical Account of these angels are as follows:

"Behold, I send an angel before you, to keep you in the Way, and to bring you into the place which I have prepared [for you]."
Exodus 23:20

"For He (God) shall give his angels charge over you (directions to help you in your life), to keep (protect and guide) you in all your ways (in whatever you do)."
Psalms 91:11

"My God has sent his Angel, and has shut the Lions' mouths, that they have not hurt me...."
Daniel 6:22

"Then the Devil (adverse thoughts and feelings) left him... and angels ministered to him (assisted him)."
Matthew 4:11

These "Angels of the Lord" have helped countless millions of people throughout the ages—and are still doing so today. When we are in a life crisis, and we are reaching out for Divine Help, these angels are ever prepared to come to our rescue, if we will only allow them to do so.

Archangels

According to general Esoteric Teachings, the Archangels are seven in number. In addition to being the directors of legions of angels, they are believed to rule over several kingdoms that regard humankind. The archangels govern the influence of seven planets, that in turn govern the twelve Signs of the Zodiac. The seven archangels also govern the seven days of the week, according to esoteric teachings. The tables of these accepted facts are as follows.

The Archangels of the Planets

ARCHANGEL SAMAEL influences the Planet Mars, and is of special help to those born in the Sign of Aries, and Scorpio;

ARCHANGEL HANIEL influences the Planet Venus, and is of special help to those born in the Sign of Taurus, and Libra.

ARCHANGEL RAPHAEL influences the Planet Mercury, and is of special help to those born in the Sign of Gemini and Virgo.

ARCHANGEL GABRIEL influences the Moon, and is of special help to those born in the Sign of Cancer.

ARCHANGEL MICHAEL influences the Sun, and is of special help born in the Sign of Leo.

ARCHANGEL SACHIEL influences the Planet Jupiter, and is of special help to those born in the Sign of Sagitarius and Pisces.

ARCHANGEL CASSIEL influences of Planet Saturn, and is of special help to those born in the Sign of Capricorn, and Aquarius.

Days of the Archangels

It is believed, in Esoteric Circles, that the seven archangels have more power on certain days of the week. They are as follows:

SAMAEL—Tuesday;
HANIEL—Friday;
RAPHAEL—Wednesday;
GABRIEL—Monday;
MICHAEL—Sunday;
SACHIEL—Thursday;
CASSIEL—Saturday.

Prayer with Fire to the Archangels

Many initiates believe that effective prayer can be made to the archangels for help in life, by using two important things: the first is to check, by the tables above, the Archangel that influences your life by knowing your Birth Sign. The second is by burning a candle, the color of which correspondence to the Archangel under consideration, and doing so on the day (or night) of the week that the power of the Archangel is most effective as given above. What follows is a brief list of the colored candles to use.

ARCHANGEL SAMAEL—Red;
ARCHANGEL HANIEL—Green;
ARCHANGEL RAPHAEL—Orange;

ANGELS OF THE LORD

ARCHANGEL GABRIEL—Light Blue;
ARCHANGEL MICHAEL—Gold;
ARCHANGEL SACHIEI –Violet;
ARCHANGEL CASSIEL—Dark Blue.

You may obtain colored candles at your local Spiritual Supply Shop or gift/variety stores. It is wise to light the candle and meditate in silence for several moments. Then write your requests on a small slip of paper and ignite it from the candle flame. Place the burning slip of paper into a fireproof dish, incense burner or ashtray. As it burn, hold the thought that your requests are passing from the physical dimension and into the spiritual dimensions of the archangels. You may utter your prayer aloud if you wish. After your prayer, go about your daily business, knowing you have placed the matter in good hands. Watch for opportunities that present themselves in your daily life that will bring you closer to achieving your goals.

Master Teacher Angels

From the perspective of our advanced thoughts, evolved humans, known as "the Ascended Masters" guide us through the portals to Higher Wisdom. These messengers communicate with rare teachers who work in the outer world—teachers who have attracted their attention and have proven themselves fit for channeling one or several of these Masters, and have the ability to transmit their teachings to the public effectively. The purpose of the Master Teacher Angels is to prepare sincere people on the true Path toward Spiritual Freedom to achieve the Ascension, also known as the Great Liberation. This, in turn, leads the pupil of wisdom to freedom from the cycle of rebirth and karma, according to the teachings of the Masters of Wisdom. The Master Teacher Angels have also been termed "the Mahatmas" by some schools of philosophy.

Angels of the Spirit World

When people experience that which has been termed death (or transition by some schools of thought), they enter the Fourth Dimension, most commonly called the Spirit World and the Astral

Plane. The word "astral" means "a star," and is connected to the human emotions that come from the Soul of Man/Woman. In the Astral or Spirit World there are several levels of evolution, from the lowest—which correspond to those people who vibrate emotionally to subhuman frequencies, to the highest heavens of that dimension—which correspond to those people who vibrate to the highest emotional aspirations of love and peace.

Souls who inhabit the Spirit World are constantly evolving—and one way in which they do so is by becoming a "SPIRIT GUIDE" to people who still abide in the physical dimension. By helping us who are still within the confines of the material world, they may progress higher in evolution within the Spirit World. There are a number of ways in which Spirit Guides communicate with us during our lives: they may give us flashes of intuition that will save us from danger, avoid an accident, or lead us to a good book or a living person who can help us in life, and the list could go on ad-infinitum. The Spirit World has also been termed "the Summerland" by Amerindian Mystics and Spiritualists.

Angels Among Us

Angels, of the various descriptions just given, have been known to walk among us. In the case of the Archangels, they manifest here only as "hologram"-type images, since their vibration is too intense to manifest as they really are within the murky levels of the physical dimension. Archangels have been known to blend with the "Higher Self" aspects of advanced human souls within the material world. Even the angels of heaven who work under the direction of the Archangels have been known to appear to people and are known as "Angels of the Lord" among most schools of thought.

Messengers from the Master Teacher and Spirit Guide Class of angels have been known to materialize a human type form that would actually be felt by the human touch, seen with the human eye and heard with the human ear. These materialized forms have been known to consume food and beverages— just like any human still in physical form—then vanish like a mirage. The one exception is that a mirage does not leave partly used food and drink, and this is exactly what happens in a case like this, as though it were a sign that some very real entity was indeed present. It is a well-known fact among Spiritualists that a medium may be able to produce the correct energy for a Spirit Guide to materialize a physical-like form within the séance room.

Another example of angels among us may be found in the many accounts of living people who ministered to people at a distance, and actually appeared in tangible form to give someone a message, even though the human angel's physical body is someplace else. This has been termed bi-location. In such cases, the human angel may know the person at a distance, or they may, under the direction of their spirit guides, be sent to a stranger. They are not always conscious of this, but may actually meet the stranger, or receive testimony from someone they know, at a future time.

Some of the angels who walk among us are people from other planets. These people have been visiting our planet in their starships, most commonly known as Unidentified Flying Objects (UFOs) for ages. Their mission is to help evolving planets exist in Universal Brotherhood and Sisterhood, in unity and peace. On occasion, they have been known to communicate with earthlings, either telepathically or in person, and their spacecraft have been viewed in our atmosphere by millions of people, from average people to law officials, to military personnel.

There has been a cloud of secrecy to cover up the existence of interplanetary explorers and messengers. There has also been a great deal of false propaganda, because of misguided channels, as well as Hollywood versions of films portraying Interplanetary Aliens as fiends. Any thinking person realizes that if beings, having such technology, wanted to harm us, they would have done so a long time ago. However, let us not ignore the other side of the coin: There are, in fact, some aliens who seek to control humanity, but the majority of them are working for the betterment of our planet.

Many of the benevolent Space Brothers and Sisters walk among us incognito, posing as normal earthlings, and have been angelic messengers to several people or entire groups.

My Personal Experiences with Angels

As a child, while receiving inspirational dreams and visions about my future work, beings from Angelic Kingdoms would appear in my room at night before I drifted off to sleep. These Angels of the Lord seemed almost like mists, but could be perceived with the human eye. They always brought comfort, peace and fortitude with their presence, as well as the promise of things to come that would mold my life.

ANGELS OF THE LORD

Later in childhood, human messengers who claimed to be affiliated with Ascended Master Teachers began to come into my life. There were several such visitations, so isolated that the different people could not possibly have known each other. Yet, they all seemed to have one thing in common—they knew the deepest questions in my heart, which I did not disclose to anyone, and they gave me the answers, along with special instructions to follow until the next visitation from such a person. During this period of life, I received a very notable materialized vision of Buddha and Jesus. Throughout these years of angelic visitations and visions, I was directed to the right books that would awaken the correct abilities to enable me for my life's work.

Visit From An Angel

On a snowy day right after my 16th birthday, three knocks came to my mother's door. We lived in the middle of the block in a string of row houses, as this was the common residential structure of dwellings in most of Philadelphia. She looked through the window and asked me to open the door to find out what the visitor wanted. As I opened the door, a tall, well dressed man stood before me. Although it was snowing heavily, his image seemed to be untouched by the snow. He wore expensive clothes, as though he were a chief executive officer in a large corporation. His hair was a silvery grey, such as I had not seen before or after. For a moment, he just looked keep into my eyes as though he were communicating an unspoken message. Then the silence broke as he asked if he could come in for a sandwich and tea, so that we could talk. I asked my mother if it was all right, and, although she was normally not given to inviting such a person into the house, she agreed in a strange manner, as though she were in a trance.

I invited the stranger in, and he quickly suggested that we go to the kitchen, where we could converse privately. Once seated, I asked him what he would like to eat. He replied that a grilled cheese sandwich and a cup of hot tea would be sufficient. As I prepared his food, I noticed that he removed a small notebook and pencil from his overcoat and began writing something down.

As the food was set before the distinguished gentleman, he requested that I sit with him. I observed how he blessed his food by placing his hands—palms down—over the plate and thanking Divine Providence that he should fulfill two missions in one day. He then began to break the sandwich in small pieces, and consuming it a piece at a time. This is when I really noticed something strange: there were no crumbs on the planet where he broke the bread, even though the sandwich was crisp. He only partially finished his sandwich and tea, then gently pushed the plate and cup aside, used his napkin, then began to write in the small notebook again. After this, he folded his hands together on the table and fixed his gaze upon me for what seemed to be a moment, yet an eternity.

He began speaking about the dual nature of my upbringing, mentioning personal things that I cannot go into in this article. He warned me of both the blessings and the burdens that I would have to endure in life. He spoke of my mission, then suddenly stopped to write in the small notebook again. He then told me that he had to go to someone who was about to depart this world a few blocks from where I lived, but had to make a stop to see me first. The person about to experience transition was obviously under his consideration and guidance. With that, he announced that it was time for him to go. He took the pencil and put it back into his overcoat pocket, but left the notebook on the table.

Unspoken Blessings

As he left, he turned to give me a final unspoken blessing, and just then I realized that he left his notebook on the table. I quickly went to get it and as I opened the door I received a real shock. I happened to look down before stepping out on the porch, and noticed that there was not a single footprint on the deep snowdrift, even though it had only been a few seconds since he walked out the door. I ventured out on the porch and partially down the dozen steps that led to the sidewalk, and there was not a single footprint, not on the porches of our neighbors; the steps and sidewalks were totally void of footprints, even though no new snow had fallen sometime before or during his visit—it was as though he vanished into thin air the moment I closed the door. I began to flip through the pages of the small notebook he left, and discovered that he had left it for me, as it was replete with personal instructions for my preparation of the work I was soon to begin publicly. Was this man an Angel of the Lord? One thing is for sure: he was a special messenger sent to guide me on the Path.

About a year later, I was suddenly awakened out of sleep. As I sat up on my bed I was startled at the sight of a man clothed in the garb of the traditional appearance of one of "the Three Wise Men." Out of the corner of my eye, I noticed two other people in the room. However, I could not turn my head to look at them; it was as though my face was set on this one man in front of me. He spoke words of encouragement, and then he opened a large book with profound answers to many of life's mysteries written on its pages. The visitor informed me that whenever I needed an answer to help someone in need, the knowledge and wisdom that I had gazed at so quickly would come forth from my Higher Consciousness. Then, with a few closing words and the passing of his hand, as though making strange symbols in the air, they vanished. Later on, it was revealed that these three visitors were the Ascended Masters Count St. Germaine, El Morya, and Kuthumi. This was positively an example of a visitation by Master Teacher Angels.

I was about ten years old the first time I can recall seeing an Unidentified Flying Object: on one of my usual nights of gazing at the stars in contemplation of the Divine, I noticed three UFOs in a triangular formation, maneuvering in the night sky. Suddenly they moved at high speed and disappeared.

While visiting the State of Missouri in 1967, I took an evening walk for some fresh air. As I stopped on the sidewalk to look up at the stars, I noticed four different colored disk-like objects. They were far enough apart from each other as to appear to occupy the four corners of the visible sky. Then they all moved toward each other, and when close enough to form the outline of a square they seemed to vanish, as though they flew straight ahead and away from earthly view at a tremendous speed. The next morning newspaper said that several people in the area had reported sighting UFOs the night before.

In early 1970, while serving as the minister of a church in Ohio, I was driving back to my apartment after an evening service. There was a bright red object in the sky, which seemed to be following me. When I had to stop the car because of traffic, the object also stopped. When the car began to move again, the object also moved. This continued up until the turn to enter the apartment complex, and then the object mysteriously vanished.

In 1981, while visiting out-of-state relatives, I was up late answering personal correspondence. Out of nowhere, a loud sound was heard outside the window of the guest room, and a very bright light beamed through the window. Suddenly, what appeared to be a shadow of human form stood between the window and the bright light, and I heard the voice of a man speaking in what seemed to be a foreign language—but the curious thing was that his words were being translated into English through mental telepathy, in bold and powerful words within my consciousness. The being identified himself by name—ASHTAR. The entire message was for a man who had some experience with UFOs, and I was to deliver the message to him on my return to Philadelphia. As it turned out, the man received the message with tears in his eyes because of things communicated by Ashtar, that the man had not revealed to another living soul.

A Special Mission

While teaching a series of metaphysical classes in Los Angeles in early 1983, another outstanding demonstration from Ashtar took place: he predicted that the Los Angeles area would experience a tidal wave that would destroy Santa Monica Pier, an earthquake, and a tornado—all in one day. He instructed me to write down, seal and give this prediction to a few of my more advanced students, who were to do special work along with myself to help cushion the impact of what was to come. All of the things mentioned came to pass, and would have, no doubt, been more severe, if not for the help of Ashtar and his fleet of spacecraft.

A special student who lived on the West Coast owned and operated an employment agency. One day, while in prayer for her, I was guided by Spirit to assign a special Angel or Protection to be with her at all times. However, I was instructed not to inform her of this angel. She was in the habit of working late, since she could not afford extra staff at the time. One evening as she left the office building, she was suddenly confronted with a would-be robber who pointed a knife only a few inches from her throat. She said his eyes looked like one possessed by evil spirits. Suddenly, the man looked over her right shoulder. As his expression changed to one of fear, he said, "I'm gone, man," dropped his knife on the sidewalk and took off running in the other direction. She turned around quickly and caught a glimpse of a bright light that vanished as she turned around, and saw no one there.

In 1980, while teaching a series of classes in Philadelphia, a certain business woman was in dire need of extra capital to expand her business. She gave a sacrificial donation to help further my work in the area, and without her knowledge, I assigned an Angel of Prosperity to assist her. On another night after class, she left for her locked car in the parking lot next to the meeting hall. When she unlocked her car and got inside, she discovered an envelope on the floor. On the envelope the words, *"Angels do exist"* was written in strange colored ink. She opened the envelope and discovered money inside. It turned out to be three times the amount that she actually needed.

ANGELS OF THE LORD

Angel of Protection

In 1967, a businessman who was also one of my students, was preparing to go to the airport for a business trip. He asked me to offer special prayers on behalf of the deal he planned to close. When I did this, I was also guided to assign a special Angel of Protection to him for some reason. As it turned out, on the morning of his departure, everything seemed to be going wrong: he was unable to get a ride to the airport on time, something was wrong with the locks on his luggage, etc. At first he became aggravated at all this, but finally resolved to take a later flight. When he did arrive at the airport, he discovered that the plane he was to board originally had crashed shortly after take off. He was spared his life because of his Guardian Angel.

While conducting classes in San Francisco in 1972, a woman from Barstow determined to drive to the Bay Area to hear me in person. She had called the center where the classes were being conducted and informed me of this. We said a prayer together over the telephone, and I felt guided to assign an Angel to guide her over the nearly 250 mile Journey. It turned out that she had very little money for the trip. She stopped for a sandwich on her way, and eventually had to stop for some gasoline. That's when she discovered that she had lost her wallet when she stopped before. She was stranded without a penny to her name. All she could do was pray. Suddenly, a man in another car pulled up in front of her, got out of his vehicle, walked up to her window and asked her what was wrong. After she told him of her misfortune, he just smiled with deep compassion in his eyes and said, "turn your car on—just do it!" She did so without question, and immediately noticed that her gas tank showed it was on full. When she arrived at the class, she gave an account of this event, and several of the students were moved to give her donations so that she could make the return trip.

I could go on with several other accounts of the Power of Angels of the Lord, as demonstrated in my own life, as well as students and friends. Their presence and ability to help is very real, even in this time of modern technology.

How to Benefit from the Power of the Angels

The first thing to do is BELIEVE. Do not try too hard to believe, just simply know that there has to be advanced beings from the physical to the astral to the mental and spiritual realms of existence—observation alone tells us this fact of life— there has to be some advanced order of things in and around us.

It is not necessary for us to understand the full mechanics of how these things work. For example, you do not have to be an expert to operate an automobile—all you have to know is how to turn it on and how to drive it safely. When you turn on the lights or an electrical appliance, you do not have to be an electrician to use the power. All you have to do is turn on the switch, and you just exercise that simple faith that it will work without question. This is the way that faith works. You take the plunge and know that everything will turn out fine. When you exercise this type of belief and trust, without allowing any thoughts of doubt to linger in your mind, you will receive the very help that you need—at all levels in your life.

In addition to Guardian Angels you may already have, you may have a Special Angel assigned to you. You may write me for more information about this at the address given at the end of this Chapter. Always remember—it is not wise to ask an angel for too much for every little thing that may arise in your life. You can only grow into your greatest power by using your own powers as much as possible. However, if there is a special purpose in view, according to the Master Plan, your angel can and will help you in some way, from a simple happening to as far as a spectacular event if necessary.

The Greatest Little Known Secret About Angels

As we look around us at the magnitude of human life and the wonders of the universe, we ask ourselves many questions about the meaning of it all. Any answers we receive only seem to generate more questions, and many give up on ever knowing the answer to life's mysteries. Some have had the experience of thinking they have found their reality, only to discover that it was either a step toward true reality or simply an illusion. One thing is for sure: when we are truly serious about finding our reality, we will be guided to it, and at times in a most peculiar way.

Many people, including myself, have and do look at the stars on a clear night, and this gives us a sense of kinship with something beyond the everyday reality which surrounds us. But, do the stars we gaze upon actually exist? Scientific research has revealed that any star we look at may have burnt out centuries ago: the light of that star may take many years to reach our field of vision here on Planet Earth. This is termed "Light Years," which means the calculation of how far light travels in a year. Since light travels at the rate of 186,300 miles per second, it would travel a distance at six trillion (6,000,000,000,000) miles per year. Therefore, if an astronomer said that a star was one light year away, he/she would mean that the star was six trillion miles from earth.

In figuring the speed of light and the distance from the Sun from earth, it takes the light from the Sun about eight minutes to reach our planet. There are planets revolving around our Solar Star—the Sun, yet our Solar System is just a minute particle in a vast galaxy that spans 100,000 light years from one to the other, and it is just one of a chain of galaxies, forming the universe, and this chain extends into infinity.

Philosophers, prophets and scientists of all ages have received the revelation that "Life" occurs in cycles of creation, involution and evolution, finally to return to a primal atom, only to begin the cycle all over again, and again, for eternity. This primal atom is compared to a cosmic egg. When the egg explodes, a period known as a "Cosmic Day" is active for a cycle of about eighty billion years, according to some thinkers. During this cycle the universe, along with its inhabitants, are expanding and evolving, including the human spirit.

In staying with the subject of the human spirit, let us keep the principles of involution and evolution in mind. Each one of us receives daily messages—no matter how faint—that prompts us to make an effort to grow and become better people, both in how we treat others as well as using the knowledge and wisdom that has been made available to us by enlightened souls. The name of the game is for each one of us to become an enlightened soul as well.

Universal Mind

The prime energy that issued from Universal Mind-God/Goddess, all there is, is the One Mind, and we are all part of the One Mind. Depending on how we use our cosmic abilities, we can become as evolved as we wish in any present incarnation we find ourselves, in spite of seeming restrictions around us, and we have lived in many incarnations, and may have to reincarnate again and again on this or some other night in the cosmos, until we reach the time of the Cosmic Night, when everything returns to the primal element or Cosmic egg. At some future time, when the Cosmic Egg explodes again to begin another day cycle, what we have done to improve ourselves during the previous day will determine what our starting point will be in the future Cosmic Day. Always remember, every Ascended Master, World Teacher, Angel, and even the Archangels, were once ordinary humans who worked their way up the evolutionary ladder by serious and constant effort, gaining knowledge and wisdom, and serving others.

Therefore, dear friend, the bottom line in my closing statements is this: at some point in the evolutionary progress of creation you, too, may become an Ascended Master, a World Teacher, an Angel, Archangel, maybe a God or Goddess. All things are possible to those who believe. However, you must begin with who you are, what you are, and where you are. Remember, an angel is a messenger.

THE ANNUNCIATION
And the angel said unto her, Fear not, Mary: for thou hast found favour
with God...(Luke 1:30)

Chapter Thirteen: More Visits from the Angels

Victoria E. of Washington is a frequent reader of our books, and so she did not hesitate to write in about her visits from angels as well as her history of paranormal experiences. Here is her story in full:

My first psychic experience was when I was in boarding school back in the twenties. Several times I would see all the questions that was going to be in the exams on the subject we were to have the next day in a dream. My seat was right in front of our instructor's desk. Often he would mark his book, when students did not know the subject matter that day and say under his breath, "mmmm, you will see that again." I would mark mine and copy down in my notebook just what to study.

That day, while trying to cram for the exam next day, I would see all the questions in a dream. I would immediately awaken, write the answer to the questions and go back to sleep. Next day, when the questions were put on the board, sometimes my tenth answer would be his first question. I would throw my pony in the wastebasket and, by the time he finished writing the questions on the blackboard, I would be finished. The same thing would happen with most of my studies.

Later that same summer, I dreamed I was visiting a friend and there was a gentleman visiting her home that she introduced to me, and some of the things mentioned in the dream happened two weeks later, when I actually met the gentleman face to face.

The next experience I had when I was living in Columbus, Ohio with an aunt (who was a medium) and was cruel to me. That night I prayed the twenty third Psalm and dreamed of my mother. All I could see was her face in a red cloud mist. She said, "Don't worry baby. Mother will get you away from here. Two weeks later, my cousin who lived in DC, then wrote me and asked if I would like to come to Washington. I wrote back that "Yes, I would." She sent me Railroad fare and I came here.

When I was about 22 years old, I was very unhappy and prayed one night to die. I always knew it was wrong to commit suicide, because God gave us life and we are supposed to wait for Him. It was during the years of the Great Depression and things were tough. I had a beautiful vision. I saw my grandmother, mother and many others all in white. I asked, "Mother is God ready for me yet?"

She only smiled.

Again I inquired, "Has Saint Peter got my name down on his book. I've tried to be good?"

Again, she only smiled, and Jesus appeared in all His light and glory and touched me and said, "Now my little one, what do you want?"

I replied, "Health, happiness and success." They all smiled and disappeared.

I opened my eyes and there was the most blinding light in my room. More bright than the sun glistening on a fresh snow after a snowy night. It was so beautiful. After I went back to sleep that night, in a dream my mother led me by the hand to a dentist. He diagnosed my mouth as having five cavities, then she led me to a doctor. His diagnosis was, "My child, your blood pressure is so low I don't see how you live."

Two weeks later, I went to a doctor and dentist and the diagnosis was identical to the dream.

There is life on the other side. We do not always see them, but some of our relatives who have passed on are our guiding angels. For 20 years, I operated my own taxicab, and quite often people who were psychic would get in my taxi, they would look on the back seat, change their minds, and sit beside me on the front seat. One woman inquired, "Your husband died, didn't he?"

I answered, 'Yes."

She said, 'You do not have anything to fear, because he rides with you every day."

In November 1978, I was robbed. There was a gun pointed at my neck, the trigger was pulled, and the gun did not go off. They got out and ran. I was hit on the head after the gun would not go off and had to have a couple of stitches in my head. After that, I stopped driving the taxicab. I asked God for something else to do to supplement social security.

Chapter Fourteen: Angels Among Us

Susan Gordon is an energetic young woman with many friends and contacts in the music and entertainment fields. With the open mind found in a growing percentage of our "baby boomer" population, she is quick to understand that the "Material World" is not the only existence and that, to some of us, angels can be as real as humans, despite an attempt by the more "stable elements" of our society to eradicate them back to a shadowy existence. Here is her story:

Almost two years ago, I sat on the steps of my domed art studio near Phoenix, Arizona, and stared at a narrow, nine-foot tall, blank canvas. It was propped against the awning of the strange little underground structure, its white surface glaring back at me as I wondered what to paint on such an odd-shaped frame. In a moment of perceived inspiration, I didn't even notice that the shadow of a nearby tree disappeared from the canvas, while a figure appeared ON it! It was only after I snapped back into reality and had already headed towards the house to grab my sketchbook that I stopped in my tracks and acknowledged what had just happened. On looking back at the tall stretch of canvas, the shadow of the tree was back and the ghostly figure I had glimpsed was gone. I retrieved a sketchbook and returned to the studio, drawing the outline of an angel that was perfectly proportioned to my nine-foot, former-dilemma.

I worked on her for months...a glowing, cobalt-blue being encased in a white sheath that ends in a cascade of feathers. She stands on a puff of clouds against an indigo background. Her face, although featureless, is often determined by observers to be the Madonna. Her head is surrounded by nine balls of light. She's painted in layers of glazed oil colors—and for the time she stood in the domed art studio, seemed to transform it into some kind of cathedral. On the day I finally decided the painting was finished, large thunderclouds gathered while I added the last touches of highlights. As had been the case over the past couple of years (since I'd started to paint "space vehicles"), on the day I completed a canvas, there would be a spectacular lightning storm. This picture was no exception, and before I could finish cleaning my brushes, we had to turn off computers and "batten the hatches" while a large electrical storm danced all around our Paradise Valley ranch.

Paintings are a language, with a life all their own.. .and it is the responsibility of an artist to inject the qualities of such language into his/her artwork. The great paintings have been known to radiate measurable energy, producing feelings of awe and grandeur in the viewer. Presumably they touch the unseen, but equally determinable electric body of man. This, too, is the work of angels, to present pictures in the human astral body. In this way, they shape the evolution of our social life—in present time and for the future. All through history, the most profound art has become reality. The fourteenth century was such a turning point in the evolution of mankind's intellect, where angels spoke through artists, and were heard by many. As we approach the beginning of the third millennia (the year 2000) such a dramatic evolutionary event is happening once again. This is the epoch of the Spiritual Soul... where we now have the opportunity to fully respond to the pictures that have been placed in our astral bodies. It is the call for global and universal brotherhood —where we will be able to see.. .not in theory, but in full, waking consciousness, the divinity in every other human being. This evolutionary step, however, is not without some hindrance, as its manifestation relies on the rational, thinking ability of the individual.

Astral vision is not achieved unless a specific effort is made to do so. For someone who is aware that this mass awakening must take place, it is very frustrating to realize that most humans are asleep! Completely unaware of great world events, small miracles in their daily lives, and much less of their true, spiritual natures. Many of those who have acted on images from the spiritual world (which is quite different from our physical existence) panic, and are diagnosed with illnesses such as schizophrenia, then are given drugs to stop the "hallucinations." Recently, the mother of a teenage "schizophrenic" told me her psychiatrist said the angels are the most popular "delusion" in North American culture. Imagine if YOU were an angel, trying to get through to humans, who, upon finally developing the abilities to work with you, were given mild-altering drugs instead of help in fully understanding the nature of spiritual communication.

Some humans, especially more and more young people these days, are self-medicating with illicit drugs. This is a very disheartening practice for angels to deal with. The central nervous System is our link to astral consciousness, and when it has been damaged by the use of drugs (that includes alcohol, which is a very toxic and dangerous substance), the human being is then unreceptive to soul vision. Unfortunately, this is a sad fact of life on our planet today...where far too many of us have fallen victim to conspicuous consumerism and medical mania. We live in a social structure where it is practically fashionable to be sick with the disease-of-the-day. And the children—so many frightened, ill, but very perceptive children—wise beyond their years and wondering why their parents can't see the truth about our shaky physical existence. Who's going to help them understand? Who's going to win the battle—automatons or free men and women who, by choice, oppose the darker forces?

We've already passed the point where angels could get their message across on the plane of waking consciousness. They work through sleep now, as the brain must be in a state known as THETA to receive the angel's pictures. It has led to a few changes in the divine plan, and some unfortunate disruptions in social evolution. For many people who do understand the angel's work, there will be no peace in the enjoyment of happiness, until others around us are happy too.

This is the point of time where we now stand. Some may call it Armageddon, some may say it's The Judgment...some may just try to pass it all off as a world gone crazy, while others toy in the labs, creating new designer drugs intended to fashion mental functions according to some textbook source of behavioral normalcy. Some may return to their couches in darkened rooms, never venturing past their favorite channel or sports page.

I say the Christ HAS returned to earth. What we create in our minds will quickly become reality, and it is up to the individual to determine what that reality will be. Luciferic and Ahrimanic forces will continue to try to stop the impending Spiritual Event. As much as angels are trying to work on physical bodies during sleep... "sleep disorders" are now a marker for mental illnesses whose symptoms often include visions of angels—both good and bad. Our best ally is our own ability to THINK, to LEARN, and to perceive the world around us correctly

Meditating on correct perception of the angel's pictures is an exacting science that requires effort and discipline, and carries with it the reward of clairvoyant thinking. Even the advancement and correct use of technology depends on our personal state of mind. How few of us really know how the body functions at its cellular level—and how the brain processes chemicals and electrical signals related to every thought and movement. It is time to KNOW ourselves as we really are, and get around the unhealthy illusions put before us. Then, and only then, will we have the tools necessary to transcend the confusion and unhappiness that currently engulf so many wonderful beings.

And please—feel free to talk to my paintings!"

Musician, writer and painter, the talented Susan Gordon of Phoenix, Arizona, believes from personal experience in the Kingdom of Angels.

Chapter Fifteen: Beings of Great Beauty

Best selling author Brad Steiger has long known of the existence of interdimensional forces as he, himself, has had brushes with such entities almost all his life. Here he recounts some of the experiences of those he has come in contact with while researching the subject of angels:

Most men and women who perceive the physical activities of angels have described them as entities of great beauty. Many percipients are able to describe the angelic apparitions in great detail, including their eyes, hair, wearing apparel and other attributes and accouterments. In the following accounts, we will note that the angel was not robed in white, as so many of the holy dead and sacred figures are so often reported to be clothed.

Dr. Eugenio Itzca (not his real name) of El Paso, Texas, wrote that in 1984, he had just delivered a baby for a poor family, and he had declined the 25 dollars which had been offered to him by the father because of the man's obvious poverty.

Dr. Itzca was headed home on horseback when the animal stopped, head erect, nostrils wide. The horse's body began to quiver, and its eyes bugged as if it were seeing something yet invisible to the man on its back. The horse began to whinny "oh, so strangely," as they seemed to be coming closer to "it."

Then the doctor saw a wonderfully beautiful being on the road before him. It was human in form with golden hair and a youthful face. Its garments were a celestial green and a soft, golden aura enveloped its form. Its eyes were blue and magnetic. It did not speak, but Dr. Itzca later said that the supernatural being answered questions in the "God-mirrored glories of its eyes."

The horse once again started walking, and the angel kept pace beside them. Dr. Itzca closed his eyes to thank God for the experience, and when he opened them, the angel had gone.

Dr. Itzca has often expressed the wish that everyone could have seen the beautiful angelic being.

"No one could ever again be materialistic and earthly after having such an experience," he said. Without trying to express a sentiment that would seem unhumble, the doctor commented that he felt inwardly that there was some correlation between the act of kindness which he had performed for the poor family and the appearance of the Heavenly Being.

In his book **Heaven and the Angels**, H.A. Baker recounts many stories of dramatic interaction on the part of angels.

Baker tells of a Chinese Christian who, during a Japanese attack on his city during World War II, was moved bodily by an angel three times from places where bombs were about to explode.

He also relates the account of the angel who pushed back a German tank during World War I in order to save many human lives.

Another of Baker's reports deals with a five-year-old boy of Angelholm, Sweden, who was lost in the woods for six days while four hundred people searched for him.

When he was found, the child said, "At night I looked up to the stars and prayed to God to help me get home again. I often got cold, but whenever I did, an angel would come and put its arms around me to keep me warm."

In a letter, a Mr. Gunderson described the following visitation:

"I saw three separate clouds float through the doorway into the room where my wife lay dying. The clouds enveloped the bed.

"As I gazed through the mist, I saw a woman's form take shape. It was transparent and had a golden sheen. It was a figure so glorious in appearance that no words can fitly describe it.

"The beautiful entity was dressed in a long, Grecian robe, and there was a brilliant tiara on her head. The angel remained motionless with its hands uplifted over the form of my wife, seemingly engaged in prayer. Then I noticed two other beautiful angels kneeling by my wife's bedside.

"In a few moments there appeared above the form of my wife a spirit duplicate lying horizontally above it. It seemed to be connected to her body by a cord.

"The whole experience lasted for five hours. As soon as my dear wife had taken her last breath, the three angels and the spirit form of my wife vanished."

Mr. E.B. Bunzel, who is now forty years old, has stated that he began to become conscious of an angelic presence guiding him about seven years ago.

At first, Bunzel experienced a number of warning dreams in which an angel would appear to direct him away from certain dangerous decisions. Bunzel stated that the angel had come to him after a year of intense prayer to God for special guidance.

Currently, according to Bunzel, the angel comes to him every morning at three o'clock and awakens him to pray. The angel has often prompted him to give to charity, and Bunzel states that he has never suffered on account of his gifts. Rather, he has become more prosperous.

Once when Bunzel was informed that he was in great peril, he prayed all night. Before dawn, he saw the angel as a form clad in white and having a countenance "admirable and lovely to behold."

When he was told the danger had passed and he was preparing for some rest, Bunzel heard a voice saying, "He that sitteth in the tabernacle of the Most High need never be afraid."

Mrs. J.M., who lives in a small town in Nebraska, stated that she was traveling with a group of people in a car when she was suddenly asked to take the wheel to relieve the driver. She did so, not hesitating, but she soon found that the make of the automobile made it quite difficult for her to operate. And the traffic was becoming very heavy as they approached Omaha.

As horns bellow around her and cars seemed to surround them on all sides, the woman prayed to God to get her through the traffic.

Mrs. J.M. felt a touch on her shoulder, she stated, and two luminous hands reached over and took hold of the wheel, which she quickly surrendered to their charge. Then, according to her testimony, "those skillful hands guided the car safely through the traffic and down a side road." At this point, her confidence restored, the hands vanished.

Mrs. J.M. insisted on calling the hands those of an angel. Her belief is not limited to the extent where she can imagine Heavenly beings becoming at all intimidated by the very earthly experience of driving an automobile through heavy traffic.

Ms. C.B. recalled the time when she was five years of age and was with her family visiting California's famous Bear Cave. She had ventured just a bit apart from her family, but she was about to rejoin them because she heard her mother calling that it was time to start home.

She stopped, though, when a voice like a "crystal bell" said: "Tell them to take another picture."

She looked up to see a beautiful figure with long, flowing hair, who was dressed in a silvery robe. The entity's compelling eyes reinforced its command.

In spite of the fact that her family was already in their automobile, the little girl insisted that they take one more picture. She told no one about the beautiful entity who had confronted her in a cave, but she continued to beg them for another snapshot until the family acquiesced to her pleas.

"The taking of this 'other picture' caused a brief delay in leaving the park," Ms. C.B. wrote. "If the family had left right away, we would have been on the highway just in time to have been involved in a dreadful automobile accident. We might all have been killed.

"Since that time," she adds, "I have heard the voice of this angelic figure many times. Once when, unknown to me, my father had been bitten by a poisonous scorpion, the 'crystal voice' told me before I heard of the incident and informed me that he would be all right."

In the June 1967 issue of *Fate* magazine, Sherman Lee Pompey related a most remarkable occurrence from his own experience.

Mr. Pompey wrote that he was conducting a religious service near Charles City, Iowa, when he had a sudden vision of one of the members of the congregation, a young woman, who was away on an automobile trip. He saw her approaching a very dangerous stretch of highway, and he interrupted his service to communicate his feelings of uneasiness to the congregation.

At that moment, an overpowering spiritual influence seemed to envelope the entire building. Then a commanding figure in gold and white light walked through the congregation and a voice directed: "Pray!"

All members of the congregation seemed to understand that they were to pray for the young woman who was traveling. The entire group went to the pastor's home and prayed for about 30 minutes. At that time a voice said: "It is past!"

Several days later, the young woman's husband, who had also been away, entered the church and experienced a re-enactment of his pastor's vision concerning his wife. In his version, however, he saw his wife's death as an alternate reality if the congregation had not prayed for her protection.

When the young woman returned, she was able to verify that she had been in danger at the time of her pastor's vision, but she had not realized the full extent to which she had been placed in jeopardy.

Angels appear particularly heedful of small children who are in danger. Dr. L, a retired clergyman, shared the following three incidents from his several years experience in the parish ministry:

A fellow clergyman's wife had a terrible premonition that her child had been struck and killed by a swiftly moving truck.

When she ran to the scene at which she had envisioned the horrible accident occurring, she found the child unharmed. However, both the child and certain witnesses to a near tragedy stated that a figure in white had appeared at the last moment to snatch the child away from death.

Two little girls who could not swim fell into a river, reads Dr. L's next account. A boatman set out on a rescue attempt, fearing that such an effort would be futile. But he found the two girls floating calmly in an "unnatural manner."

Some of those men and women who had watched the rescue from the shore stated that they had seen a beautiful person in white supporting the children until the boatman had overtaken them. The girls themselves insisted that an angel had prevented them from sinking.

Dr. L. also tells of a woman who was awakened from her sleep by a beautiful spirit being who told her to pray. The woman did as she was bade for several hours until a sensation of tranquility overcame her and she fell back asleep.

The next day the woman learned that at the very time that she had been praying, her daughter back in the city was trapped in a burning building. The fireman who rescued the girl stated that he had found the room all in flames except the corner in which she crouched. Standing protectively over the girl was an awesome being "all white and silvery."

Back in the mid-1920's when there was drought in much of the Midwest, Mrs. M. G. dreamed of a cool well nearer their home than the water they had to carry from a long distance.

One night a lovely figure in white appeared at her bedside and, through hand signals, bade her follow outside. There the entity pointed at a spot near the house, bent down to touch it, then stepped back as clear spring water bubbled forth.

The next morning, Mrs. M.G. found herself back in bed and with no sign of the blessed spring water. But she told her husband of the vision and showed him the spot to dig.

Mr. G. listened seriously, but he could find no indication of water at that place, and he felt the effort would be wasted if he should attempt to dig a well at the designated location.

Mrs. G's vision was repeated on the next two nights, but on the third repetition, the angelic presence did not return the woman to her bed. Instead, it turned and disappeared into the trees.

When Mrs. G. awoke, she found herself lying on the ground, and she cried out in fear.

Her husband found her in a distracted state, and he promised to dig at the place which the angel had indicated on three occasions.

Mr. G. had dug only a little way into the ground when he struck a spring of clear, cool water.

Remarkably, the liquid proved to be a kind of mineral water which soon gained the reputation for containing properties beneficial to one's health. Neighbors began to come from great distances to obtain the water, and some claimed rather miraculous healings from imbibing the well water. Eventually, a sanitarium was built in connection with the mineral water, and many men and women testified that they benefited by drinking from the well revealed by an angel.

"Angelic Victoria"—Angel of the Accomplishment of the Divine Plan as renderd by cover artist Sharon Nichols.

Chapter Sixteen: Hit By a Car, My Guardian Angel Saved My Life

Most theologians accept the fact that we all have at least one guardian angel who protects us against harm. Guardian angels have been known to watch over the sick, guide the helpless out of potentially harmful situations, and, in general, watch over us when danger is near.

There are many recorded instances where guardian angels have proven time after time, that they can be called upon to be "good Samaritans," given the opportunity. The following TRUE story was submitted by Barbara Lynn, an artist and song writer who lives and works in New York City. Her account quite clearly illustrates the fact that we never have to walk alone.

Anyone who has ever been to Manhattan, can tell you that you'd better look both ways before stepping off the curb. If you don't keep an eye out for oncoming traffic, chances are, you are going to get "clobbered" as I did several years ago.

In the "Big Apple," cabs and cars don't come to an immediate halt like in most other cities. When a pedestrian decides to walk out into the street, it's every man, woman and child for themselves.

I had just been to see a music publisher on 57th Street about getting one or two of my songs recorded. The publisher liked my most recent tunes and offered words of encouragement. I guess, looking back now on what happened, that I must have felt a bit "light headed," as I dashed across Madison Avenue on my way to my next appointment.

No doubt, the driver of the station wagon that plowed into me had other things on his mind, and wasn't about to slow down for anyone as he rounded the corner.

I didn't have time to think, everything happened so fast. I saw the vehicle coming, but couldn't back up onto the sidewalk in time. I should have been killed, he was driving so fast. Instead, at the last second, I felt a hand grab me by the seat of my pants and the next thing I knew, I was being lifted into the air and was let down lightly on the hood of the speeding station wagon. The vehicle was traveling so fast, that it took the driver a half a block to come to a complete stop.

When he got out of the car to see if he had killed me, there I was, sitting cross legged on the hood without a scratch. There wasn't a black and blue mark anywhere on my body. And most important of all, there was no one around who could have been responsible for lifting me into the air and depositing me so carefully back down, and in a sitting position to boot.

The fact that I know I have an "invisible friend" around me at all times, doesn't worry me. The truth is, I'm happy to know that there's someone—somewhere "out there"—who is willing to give me a helping hand when I need it the most.

Chapter Seventeen: Angels, UFOs and Crop Circles

When we think of Angels in the 1990s, we have to expand our awareness to include a broader understanding of the term "angel" to include subject matter that was not available to our religious teachers in past times. John Rodgers, author of **The New Age Bible**, and editor of the Phoenix-based *Omega New Age* paper, has a fascinating understanding of all aspects of the Angelic Kingdom.

New Agers are as willing to accept the existence of UFOs, crop circles and angels, as others are to prove that these events are merely the results of mass hysteria.

There is no doubt that the planet Venus, swamp gas, mass hysteria, airplane landing lights, and errors in vision can account for a large number of the thousands of UFO sightings reported every year. But there are still a large number unaccounted for. Plus, the recent increase of sightings and the huge number of UFOs that are being caught on video leave us with no doubt that UFOs exist.

UFOs are either spacecraft from other planets, devices made by scientists on this planet, spiritual events, or products of the imagination. There are no alternatives. Every real sighting must fit into one of these categories.

Why is it that we have so many saucer sightings—increasing frequency—at this time in the world's history?

Why is it that so many crop circles are being created at this time in history?

Why? Because we have entered a New Age.

And it shall come to pass at the end of the age, saith God, I will pour out of my spirit upon all flesh. And your sons and your daughters shall prophesy, and your young men shall see visions and your old men shall dream dreams.. .And I will show wonders in heaven above, and signs in the earth beneath.

"I will pour out of my spirit upon all flesh" God says. Isn't it interesting that the symbol for the Age of Aquarius is a man pouring out water onto the earth?

This verse, which is found both in the New and Old Testament (Acts 2:17, 19 and Joel 2:28, 30) tells us that at the end of a new age—and remember, the beginning is also an end—a number of unusual events take place.

ANGELS OF THE LORD

These spiritual events include (according to the Bible) dreams, visions and prophesy. Isn't it interesting that never in recorded history has so much prophesy and visioning taken place. The only other time it was even similar to this was over 2000 years ago—the last time a new age began.

Let's look at the similarities between the end of the age today and the end of the age 2000 years old.

Archaeologist have already found hundreds of scrolls of channeled writings that were produced 2000 years ago. These hundreds of scrolls represent only a few that have been preserved over the centuries. There could be thousands of others that have been lost and destroyed by time. And today we find New Agers channeling up a storm. Thousands of volumes of channeled writings are published every year in this country.

We can read in the Bible that many people 2000 years ago also believed that the world was coming to an end. Most of the ancient Jewish people believed in reincarnation, but there is very little reference to it in the New Testament. Why? Because they believed that the world was coming to an end and there would be no time for a next life. So they didn't bother to talk about it. Today, perhaps one-third of the U.S. population believes the world is going to come to an end sometime in the next ten or fifteen years. Today we find metaphysicians—and others —predicting the destruction of the world—by atomic war, pollution, cosmic accident or some such thing.

The Bible tells about miracles and prophets abounding 2000 years ago. Today we have miracle workers and prophets, like Edgar Cayce—many of them.

Two thousand years ago there were periods of exceptional earthquake activity in which cities were destroyed and maps changed. Today that is also taking place. Long-dead volcanoes have suddenly come alive and millions of people are awaiting the major earthquake predicted to take place in California.

What we are experiencing today, and what we will experience in the years to come, is the same kind of thing that took place 2000 years ago. It is what happens every 2100 years or so, when the Earth moves from one age into a new one.

The things that we are experiencing today happen every time we move from one age into another—and the includes angels, UFOs and crop circles!

Angels—almost every society in the past 3500 years has believed in the existence of angels—there are cherubs (you now, those cute little baby angels), and seraphim and archangels and more.

ANGELS OF THE LORD

But in spite of all the references to angels in the Bible and other literature, there seems to be nothing that tells us what an angel IS!

The primary quality of matter is that it involves time and space. The primary quality of spirit is that it does not involve time nor space. Not existing in space, spiritual beings or angels cannot have physical form. They cannot have physical dimension.

As human beings, we must think in terms of time and space. We cannot easily carry anything in our mind that does not have these properties. Therefore when any human has a spiritual experience, the mind must convert this experience into terms of time and space.

And so, over the centuries, we have described angels in terms that are familiar to us.

Angels have been wearing wings (any number from 2 to 6) for about 3500 years. The reason for this is obvious: the ancients believed that the heaven (the sky) was the home of angels and everything they ever saw in the sky had wings.

But the ancients also portrayed the angels as having four faces, the bodies of animals and all sorts of characteristics we might find difficult to understand. Obviously, they were trying to describe the unfamiliar, the alien, in terms that were familiar. Artists of the middle ages, when they were attempting to portray animals from other parts of the world, tended to make everything look like some form of dog, cat or horse—animals they were familiar with.

We of the 20th century are not a rural, agrarian people. Wild animals and the growing of crops are not a normal part of the consciousness of most of us. Therefore, when we have a spiritual experience—when we see an angel—our consciousness will convert it into terms that are familiar to us.

The most powerful things familiar to urban dwellers are machines—automobiles, trains, airplanes, rockets. There is no American who has not been exposed to the ideas of science fiction. Therefore it is understandable that anyone having a spiritual experience would describe it in terms of our day. An alien being in a spaceship. We are not necessarily any more accurate in our understanding than our ancient ancestors were.

To sum up: Individuals see spiritual beings in terms of their environmental understanding. So, in each age, angels are described differently, in accordance with the teachings of that time. At one time, angels were winged animals, then they became half animal and half human, then they were portrayed as totally human, then they became superhuman, and now they are seen as aliens from outer space. It is not that angels have changed, but rather that human understanding has changed.

We are not saying that there are no REAL UFOS. We are simply saying that individuals who have spiritual experiences—those who have been contacted by angels—will likely remember these experiences in terms of our day—as UFOs.

Thus the topic of UFOs has become all muddled. Spiritual experiences are being treated as physical events and REAL UFO sightings are treated the same as visions.

If we do not make a distinction between these two experiences, we will never know the truth.

But, simply because one UFO is an internal spiritual experience, this does not mean that they all are. We are going to have to learn to tell the difference or we are going to continue in this confusion.

And it shall come to pass at the end of the age, saith God, I will pour out of my spirit upon the flesh. And your sons and your daughters shall prophesy, and your young men shall see visions, and your old men shall dream dreams.. .And I will show wonders in heaven above, and signs in the earth beneath.

Acts 2:17, 19 and Joel 2:28,30

In the Book of Revelation, John looked up into the sky and saw "wonders." And what did he see? He saw a woman clothed with the light of the sun, with the moon beneath her feet and stars around her head. Then he saw a red dragon with seven heads and ten horns. Do you know of anyone who believes that there was actually a naked woman or a dragon floating in the sky? These "wonders" were only visions—things not to be taken literally but to be interpreted and understood spiritually.

So many of the experiences that "contactees" have had, are really spiritual experiences, visions. This explains why no one else sees anything but them. Visions are not to be interpreted literally like daily events. They are full of symbolism and hidden meanings. This also is seen in much of the "channeled contacts."

When the Bible speaks of wonders in the heaven above, it can be speaking of UFO sightings—and when it speaks of signs in the Earth beneath, the Bible is clearly referring to crop circles.

Specifically, crop circles have a great advantage over UFOs, because they hang around for a long time, so that we can study them objectively. For this reason, I am going to discuss Crop Circles and whatever conclusions we reach concerning crop circles I apply also to UFOs.

Like UFOs, there are several possible explanations for crop circles: 1) aliens, 2) a very clever group of individuals, etc., 3) a government agency such as the CIA, etc., 4) a spiritual source.

ALIENS: If crop circles are being created by aliens, it seems a very complex way of doing a simple thing. Wouldn't it be just as easy to write in English or draw pictures? Of course, aliens are alien!

INDIVIDUALS: Several individuals have taken credit for the crop circles, but none of them has yet been able to explain how to do the intricate "weaving" that has been found in most crop circles. Or how to crate by hand the "bending" of the stalks. Further, with three or four circles being created in one night in different places throughout the world. It would require a large number of individuals. What would be their motive?

GOVERNMENT: Perhaps you have heard the theory that the military has some microwave device that they are testing, and crop circles are the result of it. If the circles were just circles. Perhaps. But they are becoming too complex. Why would the military want to draw so much public attention to a secret project?

But perhaps it isn't a message but is simply a sign—a sign that an age has ended and a New Age has begun!

Every mysterious event does not have to have the same explanation. Some experiences can be actual physical events and other accounts can be of a spiritual or psychic nature.

Keep your minds open and remember—the scriptures tell us that this sort of activity happens every time we move from one age into another. If nothing else, the increased sighting of UFOs, crop circles and angels tells us that we are truly in a New Age!

ANGELS OF THE LORD

Chapter Eighteen: Secrets for Contacting Your Personal Guardian Angel

Of all the principle New Age teachers of our era, Michael X. Barton stands out for his unselfish dedication in wanting to promote the mass uplifting of humankind's consciousness to higher levels of awareness and understanding.

Writing back as far as the late 1950s, Barton revealed many keys by which an individual could expand his or her horizons and contact a variety of higher intelligence, whether they be of angelic or extraterrestrial origin. Barton wrote in a practical and easy-to-follow manner, attracting many students to his works and deeds before going into seclusion.

In one of his many discourses, Barton spoke of the manner in which it was possible to open one's self to angelic beings and to make them a part of our everyday aura and environment. One method he referred to as *"Contacting Your Secret X."* His methodology can be applied today perhaps even better than ever before to bring about contact with our own—private—Guardian Angel.

Prosper and enjoy!

Secrets of Angelic Contacts by Michael X. Barton

The first step to take on the wonderful path that leads to "Higher Contact" with our Guardian Angel is this: making "X" contact. It is so important to all who are desirous of consciously communicating with these entities that I cannot overemphasize it.

What is "X"? Simply a symbol for your own highest spirit-self. It is the high-self intelligence of you.

X, as we all know, is used in mathematics to stand for the "unknown factor." The unknown factor in my own life for many long and bewildering years was my Higher Self. I was like countless other persons, totally unaware of the existence of my higher self. It is exceedingly difficult—if not impossible—to become aware of one's higher self when one's ordinary human self demands all the attention.

ANGELS OF THE LORD

In 1940, I had a most unusual and startling experience that brought me "face to face" with my unknown higher self. I was, however, a deep and serious student of the "hidden secrets" of life. My book shelf bulged with "occult" books of every description—and yet I had never touched reality.

One night after reading a chapter or two of an advanced and complicated treatise dealing with "White Magic," I turned out the light in my bedroom and went to sleep. It was my usual bedtime— ten o'clock—and sleep came quickly.

I slept for several hours. Then, at about 2:00 AM, I suddenly was aroused to full conscious awareness. Something strange and unusual was about to happen. I sensed that what was about to occur would be of deep soul significance. In a few moments my premonition was confirmed.

As I lay where on my bed in the darkness of my little room, opening both eyes to see whatever I could in the dark, it happened. A tall, graceful being in the form of a man wearing a light flowing robe, quietly entered through a closed door and walked over to my bedside. Yes, he had walked right through the solid door and, as he stood beside me, I felt my own body begin to tremble. My eyes seemed riveted upon the remarkable being who had just "stepped into" my life in this unusual manner.

He was indeed extraordinary. Tall, well proportioned and majestic in his appearance. I had only to look into those amazing eyes of his to know, here was a being of marvelous power and intelligence. His entire body radiated a beautiful light so that I could see him easily in the dark. It seemed to me that little rays of light shone from his large eyes that sparkled like blue diamonds. The calm expression on his face indicated perfect balance of strength and love and high intelligence. And yet—I was excited and afraid.

Why? I do not know. Perhaps fear comes too naturally, too easily to the majority of us earthlings. Maybe that is why we get into fights and yes, wars, so frequently. For me, in those early days, fear was an emotion I had not yet cast out of my consciousness. I felt that emotion then.

The "Angel"—for such he most certainly was—had no intention of disturbing me further. At once he became aware of my fear and with a gentle, understanding smile upon his lips, turned around and was soon gone.

Then came a voice of my own higher self—soft but clear— "Be not fearful of your Teachers. Learn the lesson of higher love. See harmony within all creation and build a greater realization of oneness with all living beings. In this perfect love all fear is dissolved."

That was a big lesson for me to learn. And it was not until I had really transmuted fear into the higher love that the "Brothers of the Higher Arc" could reach me and teach me other important lessons. Keep this in mind as you continue your progress as a New Age Individual seeking higher contact. Love is the realization of oneness. It is the soul's sincere desire for health, harmony and happiness within all beings.

Don't, for heaven's sake, be like me—so upset that I actually "frightened" my teacher away! When your time for meeting a marvelous angelic being arrives, by all means try to maintain your composure. There is no good reason to be afraid of any advanced being who sends out the wonderful vibration of higher love to you. On the other hand, if the "harmony vibration" is missing in your contact with any being of advanced intelligence, be careful. It is possible for us earthlings to contact advanced beings who are advanced mentally but not spiritually. My advice is to always be wary of any intelligence who is "all mind, but no heart."

It is your privilege and responsibility to "test these angelic beings" before following their suggestions or advice. How do you test them? Very simply, by the trinity principles of Power, Love and Wisdom. The Lord's angels always bring about a beautiful and "balanced" effect when they communicate with you. That is because they never over-emphasize one aspect of the trinity at the expense of the other two. When they apply Power they use an equal amount of Love and Wisdom at the same time.

This causes their thoughts, feelings and actions to be harmonious, positive and joyously constructive. No matter what Teacher you contact, either on the mental, the astral, or the physical plane, test him or her for BALANCE. If you sense inwardly that he is bringing inharmony to your soul by an imbalanced vibration, this is NOT your Guardian Angel.

Regarding all contacts with angels, a word or two of caution. Never be frivolous. Frivolity is out of place, because it indicates disrespect. Communication with angelic beings is serious and of the deepest importance to you and humanity. Reaching the mind of an angel is no simple matter. There has to be a very close "attunement" of both soul and mind before the condition of rapport is achieved between you.

Here is the basic procedure to follow:

1. Wholehearted desire. You must desire to contact your Guardian Angel with a deep-souled intensity.

2. Belief in them. You must feel in your heart that these angels exist just as you do; that they can respond to you.

3. Be sincere with yourself. Ask yourself, "Why do I desire to contact my Guardian Angel?" Purity of motive and sincerity are the attitudes that will protect you from unwanted, lower entities and vibrations. They are your "shield and buckler."

4. Raise your vibration. Body, Soul, Spirit have to be raised to a new and higher level of awareness. Your awareness must rise above earth's sphere until it reaches the High Arc of Heaven.

An angel comes calling to Elijah.

If you enjoyed this book, please write to us for
our FREE catalog of books, audio CD's and
video DVDs. Don't forget to include your
name and mailing address!

Global Communications
P.O. Box 753
New Brunswick, NJ   08903

Email: mrufo@hotmail.com

www.conspiracyjournal.com

www.ingramcontent.com/pod-product-compliance
Lightning Source LLC
Chambersburg PA
CBHW081151090426
42736CB00017B/3270